WINNING
THE BATTLE
OF
THE BULGE

WINNING
THE BATTLE
OF THE
BULGE

It's *Not* Just About the Weight

MARY ENGLUND MURPHY

Winning the Battle of the Bulge
It's Not Just About the Weight
© 2006, by Mary Englund Murphy
Published by Looking Glass Press
10632 South Memorial, Suite 126
Tulsa, Oklahoma 74133

ISBN: 0-9778264-0-6

Cover Design by Misenheimer Creative, Inc., www.misenheimer.com

Photography by Ann Miller, www.chase3000.com/pagesoftime

Edited by Melanie Rigney, www.editorforyou.com

Before beginning any new eating program consult a physician.

For Bill, who thought I could do it.

For Rachel, who reminded me to keep battling.

For David, who taught me discipline and diligence.

For Jonathan, who has pleasantly surprised us all.

Table of Contents

FOREWORD

This book is an easy read about a very difficult subject—weight! And when you finish you will be armed for the battle. No question I can see myself on the pages of this book and I can see the millions of women who for over 30 years have been a part of the program called 3D—Diet, Discipline and Discipleship. God called me in 1972 to share what He was doing in my life far beyond the battle of my weight problem. And now he is asking Mary to share her honest battle of the bulge. May He bless this book and every person that reads it, and may every one of them know beyond a shadow of a doubt the incredible love of God.

Carol D. Showalter

Founder/author of 3D—Diet Discipline and Discipleship program and book

"You armed me with strength for battle;
You made my adversaries bow at my feet."
Psalm 18:39

INTRODUCTION

Have you given up, lost hope? Are you longing for a lasting change in your eating habits? Are you wondering why you're even bothering to read the introduction to one more book about weight loss? Please don't stop! I want to help you gain back the hope you've lost. Come with me on a quest that's not just about the weight.

I've been where you are now. I've been defeated more often than I'd like to admit, probably more times than I can count. I've also had great victories, reaching my goal at last, only to have my victory short-lived. Before I knew it, I was defeated once more, and those unwanted pounds were back again.

Losing weight is not just a battle; it's a war—a lifelong war made up of daily battles. Battles fought not at the refrigerator, the dinner table, or the cookie jar, but in our minds and spirits. Battles fought against an enemy we seldom recognize and with weapons we are disinclined to use. You may feel ready to surrender, but don't give up yet. Together, we will enlist in God's army, work our way through boot camp and special training, recognize our true enemy, and allow God to arm us with weapons to win the war.

A few short years ago, I was ready to give up once and for all, surrounded by the enemy. I was listening to the lies—you'll never succeed; your body was meant to be fat; don't try again because the weight will just come back; you're too old now, just enjoy the food; it's just too hard.

Just as I was ready to wave the white flag, I cried out to God in my brokenness, "Please, help me. I can't do this. I can't lose weight; it's such a battle!" Instead of surrendering to the enemy, I surrendered to my heavenly Father.

The largest land battle of World War II in which the United States participated lasted from December 16, 1944, to January 28, 1945, in the Ardennes Forest in southern Belgium. This conflict would later come to be known as the Battle of the Bulge.

Adolph Hitler believed the bond among the Allies was weak, and he could further weaken that tie with a surprise attack that would cut off supply lines and the Allied air forces. His plan depended on speed, precision, and the weather. Conditions seemed to be in his favor. The Nazis surrounded the 101st Airborne Division, and Hitler sent a message to American Major-General Anthony McAuliffe demanding immediate surrender. "Nuts!" was the response given by McAuliffe. The skies began to clear and the Allies hung on for three more days until relief came, and they were able to counterattack.

Allied Supreme Commander General Dwight D. Eisenhower stated: "By rushing out from his fixed defenses the enemy may give us the chance to turn his great gamble into his worst defeat. So I call upon every man of all the Allies to rise now to new heights of courage...with unshakable faith in the cause for which we fight, we will, with God's help, go forward to our greatest victory." Within a matter of months, the war was over in Europe.

Will you join me in rising to new heights of courage with unshakable faith in an unshakeable God? Let us no longer give in to the enemy. When he calls for surrender, we will answer, "Nuts!" We will go forward to victory!

CHAPTER ONE

THE BATTLE

"Therefore I run thus: not with uncertainty.
Thus I fight: not as one who beats the air.
But I discipline my body and bring it into subjection,
lest, when I have preached to others,
I myself should become disqualified."
1 Corinthians 9:26- 27

Chapter One

The Battle

"David, you're not even trying!" I exclaimed, squeezing the telephone receiver in my hand as I became more agitated.

"Yes, I am," he replied. I heard the frustration mounting in his voice and pictured him rolling his eyes toward the ceiling. "Mom, you just don't understand."

"I do understand. I understand you don't care about your grades. I also understand you have no idea how much a college education costs. It's about time you grow up, take some responsibility, and discipline your life." I was giving our nineteen-year-old son the same seemingly useless, semiannual lecture I'd been giving him since middle school. "You're gifted and intelligent. You're capable of good grades—great grades. I'm not even asking for great; I'm only asking for average!"

"Mom, I do care," David said. His voice lowered in defeated resignation. "It's just that school was easier for you. For me, it's a battle."

"Humph!" What did he know?

School was not easier for me, I thought, I battled too. I battled to study and develop productive work habits. It seemed to me that David battled to figure out ways to avoid schoolwork. In my opinion, he wanted the grades without the effort.

As a last resort, and with a stab at guilt, I said, "I really think you should pray about this. Don't you think the Lord expects you to use the mind he gave you to do your best? You know, the Bible says, whatever you do, do it with your whole heart."

When all else failed, I tried the godly-guilt approach. If I couldn't motivate him with sound reasoning, I would bring God into it for a final low blow. Surely, that would do the trick. It still didn't work.

No matter how hard I tried, I couldn't force David to get good grades by punishing, withholding, yelling, pleading, lecturing, praying, or extracting empty promises from him. And, his dad, older sister, and teachers all gave him similar lectures.

As aggravated and helpless as I felt, I knew David was feeling pretty much the same way. I'd seen him weep in frustration and cry out to God for help in middle school and high school, seemingly without an answer. Why was it that this child who loved the Lord, respected his elders, was well liked by everyone, and obedient to his parents simply could not discipline himself in his studies? Didn't David want to succeed? Didn't he understand that the discipline and character he developed now would mold the rest of his life? Why couldn't he just—well—do it?

After my ranting, I was as disgusted with myself as I was with David. I sighed. "David, I don't know what else to say. I know it's a battle, but at some point you're going to have to discipline yourself. You're an adult now. I can't do this for you."

In that moment, I seemed to hear a voice saying, "You know, Mary, you should think about disciplining your own life. You realize David is just like you, don't you?"

I winced. I knew that voice; I'd heard it many times before. I need to defend myself, I thought.

"I am disciplined, Lord," I said. "I have my daily quiet time, and I teach children's church and a ladies' Bible study. I'm in the church choir, and I speak at retreats. Remember me, the pastor's wife? I have to be disciplined."

"Yes, you are disciplined in some areas, but you know which one I'm talking about," he said, ignoring my pitiful excuses. "When you've disciplined your eating habits, then you can talk to David about his grades."

Although I knew David couldn't hear that conversation taking place in my head, I was nevertheless, flustered. I said quickly, "David, I have to go. We'll talk about it later. I love you."

God didn't speak to me in an audible voice, but I knew without a doubt that the Holy Spirit was convicting me about my endless years of yo-yo dieting. He was showing me I was no different than my son. David had the tools and ability to do well in school, but lacked the discipline. I, too, had the tools and ability to lose weight, but lacked the discipline to lose it and keep it off.

I, too, loved the Lord and had cried out to him in frustration many times about my weight. I wanted to succeed; I wanted to develop discipline and diligence. Why couldn't I just—well—do it?

I *was* just like my son.

David and I were both experts at producing creative excuses about why we couldn't achieve our goals; it's too hard, I don't have the time, no one supports me, I've tried before, I just can't do it.

But, I was not yet ready to acknowledge any wrong doing on my part. This is ridiculous, I thought, I'm the mother. I have the right to tell my son to shape up and start studying. I'm in control!

Oh, yes, I was in control, but all that was about to change.

Surrender

Over the next nine months, God continued to impress on me the words discipline and diligence. I refrained from nagging David too much, perhaps thinking I could escape my own guilt. But again and again, those two words resounded through sermons I heard, books I read, and even Bible studies I taught. I couldn't escape—discipline, diligence, discipline, diligence—like the cadence of a drum sounding in my head.

During that time, I reached my all-time high weight and still made excuses for my lack of self-control. I never knew my exact weight because I was too embarrassed to get on the scale, but I did know my wardrobe choices were shrinking, as I grew bigger.

I had become a pro at deceiving myself. I could pretend I didn't have a weight problem if I stayed off the scales and didn't know how much I weighed. I could blame the heat setting on my clothes dryer when I couldn't fit into my clothes. I wasn't fat; my clothes must have shrunk! I simply didn't want to take responsibility.

I starved myself for two weeks, and then gingerly stepped onto the scale. Ugh! I was disgusted with myself and ashamed to look in the mirror, yet I continued to eat my miserable way through half the summer.

One day in July, I could bear it no longer, and in tears, I cried out, "Lord, please, help me. I can't do this. I can't lose weight. It's such a battle!"

"You're right, it is a battle." That clear yet inaudible voice spoke to my heart again. "It is a battle, and you're not prepared to fight."

Oh, no, I thought, here we go again. "What do you mean I'm not prepared to fight? Of course, I'm prepared," I said, raising my defenses as yo-yo dieters are prone to do. "I'm a professional dieter, a Christian professional dieter. Over the past thirty years, I've tested nearly every diet on the market—secular and Christian." I reminded the Lord about the thousands of calories, carbohydrates, and fats I'd counted; the orchards of grapefruit I'd eaten; and the rivers of water I'd drank. And, what about the weight-loss Bible studies I'd done; I'd even taught some of them. How much more prepared could I be?

"Lord," I whined, "why don't you help me? I don't understand why you don't answer my prayers. You could take away my appetite. You could take away my desire for chocolate. I think you could make me prepared."

"Mary," he said with patience, "has it ever occurred to you that a soldier does not go into battle until he is prepared, until he is trained in warfare measures and is adept at using his weapons? It's not about me preparing. I'm always prepared. This is about your discipline and your diligence; it's about your preparation."

Ouch! There were those d words again.

"Lord, I am disciplined and diligent. And, I'm very busy. I'm busy being disciplined and diligent. You know that. I don't have time to be more diligent and disciplined than I already am," I said, talking in circles. "My schedule is hectic and filled with important—well—stuff. And, besides all the stuff I do, I pray, read my Bible, and memorize Scripture verses, even some that refer to eating. I know Ephesians 6:10-18; you know, the ones that talk about putting on the armor of God. See, I'm wearing your armor." I twirled around in an imaginary pirouette. "That's about being prepared for battle, right?"

"You're not prepared to fight the battle regarding your overeating."

This was not what I wanted to hear. What did God expect from me, anyway?

The truth is I knew exactly what he wanted. I had prayed about my weight countless times over the years, and always in sincerity, but I knew in my heart I had been asking God for a magic trick—a quick, easy way to lose weight.

It was time for some painful honesty on my part, to accept responsibility, to surrender my will to his. It was one of the hardest things I've ever done, but I made a decision that day that transformed my life.

"Lord," I prayed tearfully, giving up the argument with a broken heart, "I have no idea where to go from here, but I know you're right. I do lack discipline and diligence in my eating habits, and I'm not obedient. I'll focus on the word battle. If you'll show me what to do, I'm willing to fight."

When I acknowledged my pride and quit placing blame and making excuses for my behavior, I had remarkable peace. Why had I waited so long to give control of my body back to the one who created it? It had taken me nine months—no, thirty years—to come to the point of surrender.

"OK, Lord," I prayed, "here we go. I'm entering the battle zone. I'm crossing into no-man's-land. I will follow you as my commander in chief. I'm ready for action!"

Recognizing the Battle

The more I thought about the word battle, I actually got excited; it was a word to which I could relate. Just the sound of it made me long for combat.

Like most overweight people, I had joked about my battle of the bulge. But it wasn't very funny, and on the inside I wasn't laughing. Sure, I was in the battle—I was always defeated, always on the losing side. But now, as the Lord impressed on me the military theme, I began to think and pray about my weight in battle terms, and I saw a glimmer of hope.

Although I'd never been in the military myself, I decided to glean from the experiences of others. I recalled my father's World War II stories, my Vietnam era memories, books I'd read, and the military movies and documentaries I'd seen. I had a wealth of information from which to draw.

To visualize the comparisons, I began a list of military and battle terms I thought might be applicable to my weight-loss effort. A few that came to mind were:

Enlistment	*Enemy*	*Field manual*
Boot camp	*Weapons*	*Fellow soldiers*
Special training	*Commander in chief*	*Communication*
Cause	*Battle plans*	*Victories and losses*

Two items stood out to me—battle plans and boot camp. Both terms indicated preparation, and preparation indicated time. Wow! It was coming together. In the past, I'd never chosen a diet, thought it through, prayed about it, laid out plans, and prepared myself mentally and spiritually. Rather, I bought the latest book or magazine offering the quickest way to lose weight, and I started the program. If the results were not immediate (and they usually weren't), I'd give up.

I realized the folly of my former dieting attempts, and my focus moved in a new direction. My thoughts swam with ways to apply the other military terms. As I considered the similarities between military battles and my weight battle, I was struck with the realization that it paralleled David's battle with schoolwork, too. It became obvious why the Lord had used David to help me recognize my own shortcomings.

A Lifelong War

Few wars consist of one conflict. Yet that was my attitude toward dieting, and David's attitude toward schoolwork. I wanted to fight a few battles (diets) and be slim forever. I thought, I know it will be difficult to reach my goal weight, but when I get there, I'll be able to eat whatever I want. David wanted to fight a few battles (tests, papers, projects) and be finished with school. He thought, If I can just get through school, I won't ever have to be under this kind of structure again.

Each time I reached my goal, or came close, I gained the weight back because I quit fighting the battle. Each time David won a victory at school and raised his grades, he too quit before the next battle. David and I hadn't been willing to develop the character we needed to have lasting success in our respective conflicts. I began to understand that this war would consist of daily battles and would last the rest of my life.

God was right; I wasn't ready for war. I lacked not only diligence and discipline, but patience and endurance too. I had been looking for an easy, short-term commitment, not one that would require work and bring lasting results. I had a long way to go to change my thinking.

Like millions of others, I wanted instant gratification, particularly in regard to my body. At the checkout counter, magazine headlines drew me in like a magnet: Lose Inches, Lose Pounds; Get that Summer Body in Weeks; Learn How the Stars Keep Fit; Stay in Shape in Just Ten Minutes a Day. I bought those magazines in hopes of finding the magic diet. Instead, I found war of any kind is not easy. It is brutal, it is full of obstacles, and it is life changing, but it is not easy.

The Commitment

A week after I made my commitment to battle, we were leaving for Florida for our family vacation. We would be visiting family and friends, and I knew it would involve numerous dinner parties and eating in restaurants. I had little enough self-control at home, so I knew I would have trouble controlling myself on vacation.

I began to panic. What was I thinking? I couldn't start now! I was setting myself up for failure. Why should I put myself through the agony? I was crazy to start a new program before my vacation, particularly one that didn't even have a plan. I would tell the Lord I'd start when I got home. The trip would be filled with distractions, and I would be able to focus later. Besides, I thought, vacations are for having fun and indulging. And, what is more fun to a self-indulgent overeater than overeating?

It was tempting to retreat to my old thinking—waiting for the right timing, the right circumstances. But when is any battle fought at the right time or under ideal circumstances? No, I decided, if I'm serious about this war, my first battle will be our vacation. Now is the right time; now is the right circumstance.

"Lord, I need your help," I cried. "Help me in my battle."

"I'll be with you, Mary. I'm always with you," the Lord reminded me.

Yes, he is always with me. Although I am not always faithful, he is.

"OK, Lord," I prayed, "I'm fearful, but willing. Just show me what to do."

Just the Lord and Me!

Initially, I decided not to tell anyone what I was doing, not even my husband. I was infamous for announcing the commencement of a new diet to my friends and family. I always thought if I told people I was starting a diet, I would be more committed to sticking with it. I hoped fear of embarrassment if I failed to follow through would motivate me. But, it never worked and was painfully obvious. I had done it so many times that they had ceased listening. "That's nice," they would murmur in knowing voices.

"Good luck." Sometimes, my husband or kids would say in confusion, "I thought you were already on a diet." To them, my endless diets ran together.

No more announcements! This time, I decided, it's going to be just God and me.

Yes, battling can be difficult, but you are about to develop a purpose and clear goals; you are going to understand why you have failed in the past; and you are going to equip yourself with weapons that will defeat the enemy. You are about to emerge victorious!

Is it beginning to make sense? Will you come with me to the recruiting office? Will you say with me, "Lord, I'm ready to enlist"?

Prayer: Dear Lord, my weight has been a battle for me, and I've failed in the past. I'm now ready to acknowledge it is more than a one-time battle; it will be a lifetime war. I have not exercised discipline and diligence in my eating habits, but I am willing for you to develop those d words in my life. Thank you for being faithful even when I'm not. In Jesus' name, I pray. Amen.

Memory Verse: *"Therefore I run thus: not with uncertainty. Thus I fight: not as one who beats the air. But I discipline my body and bring it into subjection, lest, when I have preached to others, I myself should become disqualified." 1 Corinthians 9:26- 27*

Food for Thought

1. Write down what you hope to gain from this book.
2. What excuses have you made for your lack of discipline and self-control?
3. Are you viewing your battle of the bulge as a lifelong war or simply a battle until you reach your goal weight?
4. What words can you add to the list of battle terms as they might apply to your war on weight?

CHAPTER TWO

ENLISTMENT: I WANT YOU!

"No one engaged in warfare entangles himself with the affairs of this life, that he may please him who enlisted him as a soldier."
2 Timothy 2:4

CHAPTER TWO

Enlistment: I Want You!

My husband, Bill greeted the Army sergeant at the door and led him to the living room sofa. It was David's senior year of high school, and the Army recruiting office had made an appointment to talk to him about enlistment.

My patriotic heart swelled with pride to think our oldest son might join the ranks of the millions of men and women who had served the United States of America defending our freedoms over the past two hundred years. I thought of the photographs of my father in his Army uniform and Bill's dad in his Navy whites, and I envisioned David in full military dress; how handsome he would look. Why, I was ready to sing "The Star-Spangled Banner" and recite the Pledge of Allegiance on the spot!

As we sat down, and the soldier handed us colorful brochures intended to entice young men and women to enlist, I noticed the sharp crease in his pants, his tucked-in shirt, and his spit-shined shoes. My, I thought, how neat and clean-cut he looks. I glanced at his waistband and belt, noting they were actually positioned at his waist. I tried to recall the last time David's waistband had been anywhere near his waist, let alone the last time he had worn a belt.

I shook off the thought and turned my attention back to the recruiter presenting the benefits of Army life to my son. The sergeant was showing David a list of jobs that could lead to future careers after the military, and the added incentives of a cash bonus for immediate enlistment and the G.I. Bill—money for a college education.

Oh, my, I thought, with David's grades and ACT scores, this is a gift from heaven. Sign this boy up! I mentally deposited the cash bonus into a money market account and began to calculate the interest over a four-year military career. My patriotism faded into dollar signs.

I tried once more to focus on the conversation and put my motives into proper perspective, but my thoughts wandered again. Army life—ah! I pictured David in the barracks with his bed unmade—just like home. "Give me twenty, soldier," his drill sergeant would bellow, pointing to the floor and demanding pushups from our son. And would David whine, "I don't feel like it. I'll do it later, Sarge"? Oh, no! We're talking complete, instantaneous obedience.

Now my mental picture shifted to a trail of socks, underwear, and wet towels strewn across the barracks floor. "Latrine duty for two weeks, Private!" the sergeant would shout, holding out a toothbrush to David.

Ha! What a vision! David on his knees scrubbing toilets, sinks, and showers—with a toothbrush, no less! Oh, this is too delightful, I thought with sadistic glee. Free career training, cash, a paid college education, and discipline—what more could I ask? Oh well, yeah, I mean pride and patriotism, God and country. I couldn't forget those things.

The recruiter left two hours later; David did not enlist, and I did some serious soul-searching about my self-serving motives regarding our son's future.

What's in It for Me?

The reasons young men and women enlist in the armed services are numerous and varied. During times of war, some enlist out of a sense of patriotism and the desire to defend and serve their country. Others join because they lack direction, need a job, or desire to follow a family tradition.

When I made my commitment to fight my battle of the bulge, I again needed to do some serious soul-searching. This time I struggled with my motives for enlistment, for though I was headed in the right direction, I was still self-focused, as I had been about David's potential Army enlistment. I had barely made my commitment when I began to calculate my victories and mentally gather the spoils of war.

I imagined myself after a few months of successful battling. Perhaps a friend would comment on my slim figure, and say, "Wow, you look great! How did you lose all that weight?"

I envisioned a summer at the pool basking in the sun—without my thunder thighs, of course.

I pictured myself choosing clothes from the assortment hanging in my closet—clothes I hadn't been able to squeeze into for years, but that I planned to wear as soon as I got thin.

With my focus on "what's in it for me," I reverted to my old attempts at cajoling God into answering my prayers.

"Father, you know your Word says our bodies are the temple of the Holy Spirit, and I know you want me to be healthy, so please help me lose weight."

Or, "Lord, if you'll please help me lose weight, I'll tell everyone you did it. I'll give you all the glory."

And, "You know 1 Corinthians 4:2 says we should be good stewards. I know you don't want me to waste money on new clothes, so please help me lose weight."

Chances are you, too, have tried to manipulate and coax God into helping you lose weight through similar self-centered prayers. You decide what you want, find an appropriate verse to twist and back up your request, and then look forward to the desired result.

But are those prayers truly pleasing? Is that how our lives give God glory? Of course not! If we're honest, those prayers are nothing more than cheap bargaining attempts. We read the precious Scriptures, produce our own distorted interpretation, present our selfish petitions at the throne of grace, and demand our answers. That's why the Bible says, "When you ask, you do not receive, because you ask with wrong motives, that you may spend what you get on your pleasures" (James 4:3).

Honesty

"Mary, I have something else you can work on along with diligence and discipline—honesty." I knew God was quietly prompting me again.

"What?" I protested, "I am hon…" My objection trailed off. Was I really honest, or was I simply deluding myself?

I began to build my defense. How could I be blamed if my family and friends didn't support me as they should? It wasn't my fault that circumstances weren't always conducive to my diet of the week.

This time, my mental arguments were short-lived. I wasn't honest when it came to my food consumption. I ate more than I admitted and made empty promises to God, to others, and even to myself. I made absurd excuses for my failures, and my motives were anything but pure and honorable.

"Okay," I relented, "so I haven't always been exactly honest about my dieting, and I will admit to those rare occasions when I blamed someone or something else, but I enlisted to lose weight, not to be disciplined, diligent, and honest. Let's get out the weapons. When do we start fighting the battles? When do I start shedding this fat?"

"I told you to prepare for battle, and you agreed to enlist and follow me. We're going to work on the preparing part before we work on the battle part. It will take time," he told me. "And, besides, it's not just about the weight."

Time, I thought, how much time? Right now would be just fine, thank you. And, what does he mean it's not just about the weight? Of course it's just about the weight. It's about me getting rid of this excess fat!

Knowing my thoughts, he patiently said, "No, it's not just about the weight, and it's not just about you. Trust me, you'll get it."

Attitude Adjustments

To help myself better understand the military enlistment process, I interviewed men and women with experience in the armed forces. They all agreed that military service, boot camp in particular, was not wholly what they expected, and they had to make huge adjustments in their attitude and behavior. I could certainly relate to that—God was making major adjustments in my attitude, and I had a feeling the behavior part was soon to follow.

The Bible records some wise advice the Apostle Paul gave young pastor Timothy about the attitudes and behavior of enlisting soldiers and the direction they should take.

"You then, my son, be strong in the grace that is in Christ Jesus. And the things you have heard me say in the presence of many witnesses entrust to reliable men who will also be qualified to teach others. Endure hardship with us like a good soldier of Christ Jesus. No one serving as a soldier gets involved in civilian affairs—he wants to please his commanding officer. Similarly, if anyone competes as an athlete, he does not receive the victor's crown unless he competes according to the rules. Reflect on what I am saying, for the Lord will give you insight into all this" (2 Timothy 2:1-5, 7).

As I read those verses, I reflected on the differences between an enlisting soldier and a professional dieter.

- Dieters depend on their own strength and wisdom.
  Soldiers develop strength and depend on the wisdom of their superiors.
- Dieters want all the answers and demand guarantees before they commit.
  Soldiers commit to find the answers and know that victory is guaranteed through obedience.
- Dieters focus on self to gain personal results.
  Soldiers focus on others to create a team unit and develop future recruits.
- Dieters aren't interested in a sensible training process that requires time and effort.
  Soldiers know the only way to victory is through the process of intelligently planning and preparing.
- Dieters quit when the circumstances aren't "right."
  Soldiers endure hardship under all circumstances.
- Dieters want instant results.
  Soldiers know results will be slow and steady.
- Dieters want a limited, short-term commitment.

Soldiers are committed for the duration of the war.

- Dieters make their own goals.

  Soldiers make the goals of those who enlisted them their own.

- Dieters get caught up with the world's standards, expectations, and methods.

  Soldiers avoid any outside entanglements that might hold them back from victory.

- Dieters use their own weapons (fad diets, appetite suppressants, surgery).

  Soldiers use the weapons provided by their superiors.

- Dieters follow their own rules.

  Soldiers follow the proper rules of engagement.

- Dieters win occasional victories, but eventually lose ground and gain back their weight.

  Soldiers hold the line because they have patiently prepared and executed their plan.

I didn't know what to expect when I enlisted to fight my battle of the bulge, but I was beginning to understand. Are you also seeing the difference between traditional, short-term dieting and a commitment to a permanent life change? Like internment in a POW camp, dieting leads to bondage. But, you can be set free; you don't have to remain a prisoner of lifelong, professional, yo-yo dieting. In the coming chapters you will move from dieter to soldier, loser to victor. The only losing you will do is the shedding of excess weight!

I Want You!

Do you struggle with acceptance from God? Are you fearful he is disappointed in you because of past dieting failures? Are you wondering if he'll give you another chance? Are you worried that your motives may not be pure? Are you afraid of failing—again? Don't be afraid! God is the God of second, and third, and fourth chances. Bring him your doubts, fears, and past failures. He is loving and forgiving, and he is ready for you to start again—right now!

Do you remember the old Army recruiting posters picturing Uncle Sam pointing his finger straight ahead and the caption reading I want you! For the US Army! Your heavenly Father wants you; he's waiting for you—just the way you are (1 John 4:10).

You are a soldier in the Army of the Almighty God. Are you ready? You're about to begin preparation for battle; you're on your way to boot camp!

Prayer: Dear Lord, thank you for accepting me just the way I am. Forgive me for my past failures. Help me now as I build diligence, discipline, and honesty into my life. Help me as I change from dieter to soldier. I'm enlisting in your army to fight my battle of the bulge in your strength and power. In Jesus' name, I pray. Amen.

Memory Verse: *"No one engaged in warfare entangles himself with the affairs of this life, that he may please him who enlisted him as a soldier." —2 Timothy 2:4*

Food for Thought

1. List the reasons you want to enlist in God's Army.
2. List areas in which you have not been honest about your eating and weight.
3. Read again the list of differences between dieters and soldiers. To which points can you relate?
4. List attitude adjustments you need to make.

CHAPTER THREE

BOOT CAMP: YOU'RE IN THE ARMY NOW!

"LORD, you have heard the desire of the humble;
You will prepare their heart." Psalm 10:17

CHAPTER THREE

Boot Camp: You're in the Army Now!

Vikki lifted my dripping head from the salon sink and raised the back of the chair to an upright position. Throwing a towel over my hair, she twirled the chair till our eyes met in the mirror. To my astonishment, Vikki burst into tears and cried, "Mary, you've got to help me!"

What could be wrong with my dear friend? I wondered. A flood of possibilities rushed through my mind in the next few seconds. Were Vikki and Ken having personal problems? Had something happened to one of their children or grandchildren? Had she received bad news from the doctor?

Vikki is always upbeat, and I stop by her shop once or twice a week just to have my spirits lifted. Her happy face and encouraging words cheer everyone who comes in contact with her, which is why I was stunned to see my friend standing over me weeping.

"Vikki," I said, "what is it? What's happened?" Though I was sincerely concerned about Vikki's troubles, I have to admit I was a little uneasy about her cutting my hair while she was in such an emotional condition.

"Mary," she repeated, "you've got to help me. You've got to help me with my weight!"

"Oh," I said, heaving a visible sigh of relief.

I didn't know what to say. On one hand, I was thrilled that her family was intact, her children were safe, and she was not dying from an incurable disease. On the other hand, I didn't know where to begin with my own weight problem, let alone help someone else. Just three days earlier, I'd committed to battle. I had told the Lord it was just between him and me; it was our personal pact. Besides, I couldn't tell Vikki I was on my way to a spiritual boot camp. She would think I was crazy! How could I describe the things the Lord was impressing on me? Why today, of all days, did she have to bring up her weight problem, and why did she have to cry?

While Vikki dried her eyes, I did some fast thinking and praying, and the Lord gave me the answer. "You're going to need help, a fellow soldier in your battles, and Vikki is the one. I've broken her heart about her weight just like I broke yours."

Vikki silently began to comb the tangles from my wet hair. I looked at her and said, "Vikki, I don't know how to explain it, but the Lord is working in my life about the same problem. I'm not sure what I'm going to do or where this is going to lead, but if you want to get together with me after we come back from Florida, I'll tell you all about it."

"Thank you so much," she said. "It's just that I've been gaining weight, and I can't get it under control. I don't know what to do."

"It's all right," I assured her. "We'll talk about it when I get home. In the meantime, let's be praying for each other."

Great, I thought. I have two weeks to figure out what I'm going to do and then explain it to my friend.

Identifying with the Savior

"Lord, I don't know anything about boot camp," I prayed. "Where do I start?"

"Just start with what you know," he said. "Think about it, and take one step at a time."

I knew practically nothing about basic training beyond what I had seen in the movies—soldiers begin Army life by having their heads shaved and being issued a new uniform. I recalled amusing scenes of young men as they headed for boot camp. "How would you like your hair cut?" the barber would ask, and then sadistically proceed to shave the recruit's head right down to his scalp.

A haircut and new uniform are the initial means by which recruits are given a new sense of identity. It shows that the soldiers are leaving behind their old life and beginning anew in a life of service to their country. That's what I needed—a fresh start and a tangible way to identify with my new goals and vision, and that's how I ended up at Vikki's hair salon that Thursday in July. I wanted to identify with my commander in chief, the Lord Jesus Christ, and a haircut seemed like the best place to start.

Now, I thought, *what about a uniform?* The clothing choices from my closet were slim since I'd gained so much weight, and I was not to purchase any more "fat" clothes. I tried to recall what I had worn to church the last time I felt fairly confident about my appearance, and decided to wear that outfit the next Sunday. No one there would be aware I was a new recruit, but *I* would know.

It may seem corny that I took those steps, but it was important to me that I do something tangible that would give me an *immediate, visible* demonstration of my commitment. My haircut and dress were an outward expression of the inward changes beginning to take place in my heart. I was showing the Lord (and myself) that I wanted to obey him and seek his direction.

Soldiers' haircuts, uniforms, and carriage identify them as representatives of the United States, and their commanding officers count it a privilege to identify with them. That is the kind of identification I wanted to have with Christ. I wanted him to know I was sincere about developing discipline and diligence. I wanted him to know I was proud to belong to him, and I was going to take better care of my body—inside and outside!

Dieters are always looking for immediate outward results, but this time it was an immediate *inner* result I sought. Before, I let quick results and outward appearance determine the length and level of my commitment—a shallow commitment based on what I *saw* and how I *felt*. I focused on how quickly I could lose five to ten pounds and how good I looked physically. If I didn't notice an immediate reduction in the first few days of dieting, my commitment ceased.

Now, instead of focusing on unrealistic weight loss and what others would say and my physical appearance, I began to focus on: *how does the Lord want me to proceed; how can I identify with him; is my physical appearance pleasing to him?* I found the answers to those questions and more as I sought his guidance and direction, and I began to develop a closer, more intimate relationship with him.

Lord, Could You Hurry a Little?

Old thinking patterns are not transformed easily or quickly. I had my haircut and my uniform, but I was longing for action.

"I'm ready for battle, Lord," I said, "let's get out the weapons and start fighting this war!" I was eager to start taking off those extra pounds.

"Not so fast, Mary; I need to remind you of a few things. You're still thinking primarily about the weight, and it's not…"

"*Just about the weight*," I finished. "Yes, I remember."

"Good. Boot camp is a time for diligently training and learning to be disciplined and patient. The process will require time, patience, and preparation."

Wonderful, I thought, *patience—another virtue to work on.*

"Lord, I *am* patient," I said, "but could you hurry a little?"

Fortunately for our nation, our military commanders have more patience than I do. I'm comforted to know our soldiers don't enlist, get a haircut, put on a uniform, and hasten into battle. The casualties would be terrible, and our cause would be lost. Thankfully, our soldiers must be disciplined and trained until they are prepared to meet the enemy. Those in authority know the value of patience.

Many of us have been casualties of countless diet wars, and is it any wonder? We observe our fellow-dieters (our acquaintances who are also looking for a magic diet plan), and when we see them beginning to lose weight we always ask the same question, "You look like you're losing weight. *What are you doing*?" What we're really saying is, "Hey, tell me how you're losing weight. I hope it's really easy so I can do it too." Then, we run out and buy the recommended book, pills, powder, or liquid, try it for a few days and when it doesn't turn out to be as easy as we hoped, we quit. Consequently, our cupboards are overflowing with half-filled containers of various diet concoctions, and our bookshelves are crammed with partially read diet books.

Getting Down to Basics:
Preparation, Preparation, Preparation

Basic training is intended to train new recruits in the Army way of life, preparing young men and women to work as one defending our people, lands, and interests. Their new haircuts and uniforms may make them *look* like soldiers, but the following weeks of intense training will make them *think* and *act* like soldiers. They learn there is a right way, there is a wrong way, and there is the *Army way*!

Do you realize that you too have to defend yourself against attack? Do you know who or what your enemy is? Do you know who your commander in chief is, and have you learned to obey him without question? Do you know what your weapons are and how to use them? The answers to these questions and more are just ahead.

Our battle of the bulge is a real battle, a real war. It is not fought with guns and tanks, but with real weapons suited for this war. A rifle would never be put into the hands of a soldier who is not proficient in the use of weaponry, nor would a soldier who is unable to submit to authority be placed on the battlefield. Why then do we expect to win our eating war when we have not prepared and trained by developing endurance, discipline, diligence, courage, honesty, and patience, and when we have not learned to submit to the authority of our heavenly Father?

Below are some of the parallels I noticed between the boot camp training of our military and the preparedness we need before we start an eating plan.

Fears and Emotions—It doesn't take long for soldiers to question whether they will survive the intensity of basic training. Doubts, fears, and anxiety are typical responses, and these are some of the same emotions I experienced when I first committed to my weight war. You too may be questioning whether you can do it. Don't fret before you even get started! Take one step at a time, and remember you are committing to, and preparing for, a *life* and a *heart* change. It's not about you, and *it's not just about the weight*. This is about Jesus Christ finishing a work in you and through you. He's right there with you; you are *not* alone. "…He who has begun a good work in you will carry it on to completion…" (Philippians 1:6).

Identity—Just as the uniform and behavior of soldiers reflects who and what they represent, as Christians our attitudes and behavior reflect who and what we represent. When others look at your eating habits and how you maintain your outward appearance, do they identify you as one who is disciplined and takes care to represent Christ, or do they see someone who cares more about satisfying personal appetites? Your conduct and physical appearance should identify you as a soldier of Christ. How does *your* "uniform" look on you? "Rather, clothe yourselves with the Lord Jesus Christ, and do not think about how to gratify the desires of the sinful nature" (Romans 13:14).

Loneliness—Can you imagine the overwhelming loneliness some recruits feel during the first weeks of basic training? They're far from home, sleeping in an unfamiliar bed, eating different food, and physically and mentally training nonstop with scores of people they don't even know. Battling your weight can be lonely too, particularly if you are the only one in your household who needs to lose those extra pounds. Your new eating plan will probably include foods different from those the rest of your family eats, and you may feel alone in your struggle. That is why you need a person to support you in your battle. (In our battle groups, we call this person a *battle buddy*.) We all need someone who understands what we're going through, someone to lift and encourage us. In spite of my resolve to battle alone, the Lord knew I needed support, and he gave Vikki to me. "Two are better than one, because they have a good return for their work: If one falls down, his friend can help him up. But pity the man who falls and has no one to help him up" (Ecclesiastes 4:9-10)!

Giving Up Personal Freedoms—Among the disciplines soldiers learn is giving up the freedom to eat whenever and whatever they desire. Should we be any different? I'm not talking about the regimented eating schedule of boot camp, but rather the disciplines of self-denial and self-control. We often eat and live as if the world revolves around us, as if we are free to do whatever we want with our bodies. And, isn't that what the world teaches? "It's your body; do what you want with it!" Excess weight is the result of indulgence in that so-called personal freedom to eat what, where, and when we want. Perhaps you eat at mealtime, snack time, bedtime—*anytime*! You eat with friends, with family, or all by yourself. You eat because you feel good; you eat because you feel bad. After all, it is *your* body, isn't it? *No!* This is *not* your body to do with as you please. Your body is a gift from God. "…Do you not know that your body is the temple of the Holy Spirit who is in you, whom you have from God, and *you are not your own*? For you were bought at a price; therefore glorify God in your body and in your spirit, *which are God's*" (1 Corinthians 6:19-20, emphasis mine).

Structure and Orderliness—*Structure* reminds me of a regimented lifestyle, and *orderliness* makes me think of planning. If I'm going to have structure and orderliness in my life, I will have to follow instructions according to a *plan*. Isn't that what soldiers do in boot camp? They follow the orders, training plans, and schedules of their commanding officers. If soldiers went to war with no training, no structure, and no plan, there would be chaos on the battlefield, resulting in casualties.

Excess weight is the result of having no plan for victory *or* defeat. Yet again and again, I hear people say they don't understand how they attained their current weight; *it just seemed to happen.* No, it didn't *just happen.* Lack of structure and orderliness is also a plan. It's a bad plan that results in defeat. How many Fridays have you promised yourself that you will start a diet *next* week, then you wake up the *next* Monday morning with no plan or preparation. When evening comes, you are already making promises to start again *next* Monday. You just don't understand how it happened. "But everything should be done in a fitting and orderly way" (1 Corinthians 14:40).

Avoiding Distractions—New recruits' free time and leave are limited to keep them focused on training, purpose, and goals. They are taught to stand at attention and look straight ahead, neither to the right nor to the left. Are you a yo-yo dieter whose focus is easily distracted? Are you derailed by the fragrance of cookies browning in the oven, a sneak peek in the bakery window, or a child licking an ice cream cone? When your focus remains on Christ, your course will be steady and sure. In the following chapters, you will lay out plans and goals to avoid being distracted from your goal.

Physical Training—We don't want soldiers on the battlefield who will break down because they lack the stamina to continue the fight. Physical exercise is a major part of a recruit's routine. It not only gets the body in shape, but also keeps the mind healthy and alert. Are you resisting including exercise as part of your daily routine; are you ignoring its value and making feeble excuses? Are you too busy, too tired? You may not need strength for a military engagement, but you do need a clear mind and a healthy body to be a productive soldier in the Lord's army.

Brokenness—It's not until recruits are broken that they are truly effective as soldiers. I interviewed numerous former military personnel, and their insights in this area were invaluable. Let me share with you what they said.

- Basic training is a mental game. Some quickly learn to obey and follow orders, while others stubbornly resist. Eventually, they either give up (quit) or give in (submit).

- One of the primary purposes of basic training is to break the will of recruits so they will learn to think and function as one unit, not as individuals.

- Recruits have either *positive* pride or *negative* pride. The positive pride is manifested in their attitude toward their country, their uniform, their fellow soldiers, and who they are becoming. Those with negative pride are self-focused and will not submit to the orders of their superiors. They choose to function independently of the platoon.

- Recruits learn to trust the judgment of their commanding officers and to obey orders even when those orders do not seem to make sense.
- Those who finish well are not necessarily those who are the strongest physically. A positive attitude combined with diligence and determination is as important as physical strength.

Do you detect the parallels? Some of you can already see the importance of preparation, training, and developing diligence and discipline *before* you begin a new eating plan. You're way ahead of those who stubbornly resist or those looking for the easy way, still trying their old fad diets and miracle concoctions.

Are *you* broken? I don't mean simply feeling disgusted with your looks or having the pathetic yearning to look like you did in high school. I'm talking about being willing to give up control of your self-indulgent eating notions and habits and becoming one with Christ in your thinking and purpose. I'm talking about recognizing that you cannot win this battle in your own strength; that you must learn to listen to the direction of the Holy Spirit, obeying him without question. Victory belongs to those with godly character and an obedient and submissive spirit, not necessarily those with iron resolve. "The sacrifices of God are a broken spirit, A broken and a contrite heart—These, O God, You will not despise" (Psalm 51:17).

What Now?

I was overwhelmed with these new concepts, but the idea of being *prepared* for battle made so much sense that I wondered why I hadn't thought in those terms before. I still didn't have a specific plan, but I was beginning to have new direction.

"Lord," I prayed, bursting with questions, "I'm beginning to understand, but where do I start? What foods should I eat? What about our vacation? Do I start a diet plan now or wait until I get home? I know if I was really in boot camp, I'd have to make sacrifices. Should I quit eating something?"

I could sense he was prompting me again. "Good, I can see you're beginning to understand. You're beginning to understand why *it's not just about the weight.* And, yes, now that you're asking, there *is* something I want you to limit—soda."

"Oh, no!" I resisted. "Not soda!" It had been my favorite beverage since grade school;

my favorite beverage loaded with sugar and empty calories.

Silence.

"OK, OK, you're right," I said, giving in. "I drink way too much soda."

"All right," he resumed. "Limit yourself to one soda per week, and start drinking more water."

"But, what about the food; which diet should I start?" I asked.

"No more diets for you. Diets are temporary, and this is a *lifelong* war. We're going to change your eating habits for life. While you're on vacation, start cutting your portions in half, eat more fruits and vegetables, and, most importantly, spend more time with me. We're going to start preparing for battle together, and while you're in Florida, we'll start working on your discipline and diligence."

I didn't hear an audible voice, but I knew it was God impressing on me the direction I needed to take. I spent the next two weeks obeying by limiting my food portions and praying and thinking about what it would mean to battle from a biblical perspective. Verses pertaining to warfare, both spiritual and physical, began to come alive to me.

When I came home from vacation, I gingerly stepped on the scale. To my amazement, I had stayed the same weight—I hadn't gained a single pound! It was a real victory, since it was typical for me to gain at least five pounds during a two-week vacation. But I had gained something of far more value than just maintaining my weight; I was beginning to understand the lasting value of wisdom, endurance, patience, diligence, and discipline. And, yes, obedience and submission!

Vikki became my accountability partner, my battle buddy, and we began to meet every Monday afternoon. Each week it became clearer why the word *battle* had been impressed on my heart; the analogies were fitting and the Scripture verses abundant. Our focus was no longer merely on the weight (although we did weigh in each week to hold each other accountable, and we were excited as we consistently lost an average of one pound per week). Our focus turned to obedience, developing godly character qualities, and seeking what the Lord wanted to accomplish in our lives through the battle process. The rewards of a changed life and a new attitude quickly transcended the rewards of loss of weight.

Prayer: Dear Lord, I have not been patient in my weight-loss attempts, and I have wasted valuable time looking for an easy diet plan; but no longer. Instead, I will begin to prepare myself mentally, physically, emotionally, and spiritually. I know it will take time, but I am committed for the duration of the war. I want to clothe myself in Christ, identifying myself as his and being an example to others. Forgive me for allowing my eating habits to be self-centered and out of control. I know it will not be easy, but I will look to you for strength and guidance. In Jesus' name, I pray. Amen.

Memory Verse: *"Lord, you have heard the desire of the humble; You will prepare their heart." Psalm 10:17*

Food for Thought

1. You were probably motivated to read this book by a desire to lose weight. In what ways do you now view your battle of the bulge differently?
2. How can you visibly identify with Christ in your battle?
3. Are there any foods or beverages you feel the Lord wants you to limit or give up entirely?
4. What does it mean to you to be "broken" about your weight?

RECOGNIZING YOUR ENEMY

"Be self-controlled and alert. Your enemy the devil prowls around like a roaring lion, looking for someone to devour. Resist him, standing firm in the faith, because you know that your brothers throughout the world are undergoing the same kind of sufferings."
1 Peter 5:8-9

CHAPTER FOUR

Recognizing Your Enemy

"Sarah and Jennifer are not the enemy, Mary. Your focus is in the wrong place." Lea is one of those friends who tells it like it is, even when you don't want to hear it. As my good friend and mentor, she was seeking to give me wise counsel, but I was more interested in nursing hurt feelings than listening to sound Biblical advice.

"But it isn't fair," I whined. "I told you what's going on; they're making my life miserable. They gossip to people in the church and say things about us that aren't true. How am I supposed to feel? How am I supposed to react?"

"I understand you're hurt; nevertheless, they are not the enemy," Lea replied with patience. "As long as you continue to focus on the wrong enemy, you will lose the battle."

"But what they're saying, what they're doing is wrong. What am I supposed to do?"

"Yes," she replied, "what they're doing is wrong, but they are not the enemy."

"If they aren't the enemy, who is?" I asked, already knowing the answer.

"Satan is the enemy, and he wants to destroy your effectiveness for the Lord and steal your joy. You'll just become angry and bitter if you continue to focus on Sarah and Jennifer. Let the Lord take care of them. You can't change them; you can't change anyone but yourself."

I didn't feel like I was the one who needed changing, but I knew she was right. I wasn't going to *become* angry and bitter; I was already there. Each time I saw either Sarah or Jennifer, every muscle in my body tensed as I recalled things they had said and how they had hurt me. It was difficult to speak to them, and I found myself avoiding them when our paths crossed.

The counsel Lea gave me was wise. Although Sarah and Jennifer never changed or apologized for anything they said or did, *I* changed my attitude toward the situation and, consequently, toward the two women. They didn't change; I did. Once I recognized my real enemy, I focused on my weapons and battle plan, and I was able to claim the victory.

Food Is Not the Enemy

Are you familiar with the story of *Don Quixote De La Mancha*? It is about an ordinary Spanish country gentleman, Alonso Quejana, who becomes obsessed with knighthood and chivalry. Eventually, he goes mad, changes his name to Don Quixote, and rides about the country on his old nag uselessly attacking windmills with his lance that he believes are giants. For years, I fought windmills and, like Don Quixote, used my weapons ineffectively because I didn't know my real enemy.

Throughout my dieting "career," I focused on various foods, people, and my appetite as my enemies. I blamed myself—if I was a godly Christian, I would have self-control. I blamed my husband—if he loved me, he would help me control my overeating. I blamed my children—if I didn't have to cook for them, I wouldn't eat so many desserts and snack foods. And, if I'm going to be truly honest, I blamed God—if he wanted to, he could take away my desire for food and give me self-control. I also blamed my jobs, potluck dinners, thin friends, vacations, and holidays. You name it, I blamed it!

It was not until I began to see my weight problem as a real battle that I realized I would have to fight a real enemy. But, what was it? Who was it? Was it me? Professional dieters tend to have a faulty self-image, so it was easy to place myself in the enemy role. Before I could prepare for war, I knew I needed to have a grasp on whom or what my enemy was and how he worked.

I considered Lea's counsel. Sarah and Jennifer were not my enemies; Satan was the enemy. I asked myself what he was trying to accomplish in my life through that conflict. *Well,* I thought, *I suppose he would like to see our relationship destroyed and our problem could cause division in the church. And there was the matter of bitterness and anger that couldn't help but affect my relationship with the Lord.* It was clear the enemy was having victory through this conflict.

It made sense Satan would want to cause division in relationships and among people in a church, but how could he be my enemy regarding my weight and appetite? I asked myself the same question again: What was Satan trying to accomplish in my life regarding my war on weight? I thought, *I guess he would like to see similar results as those with Jennifer and Sarah. I sometimes feel angry and bitter toward others and myself, and I certainly spend an excessive amount of time obsessed with weight loss, dieting, and physical appearance. And, my relationship with the Lord regresses when I blame him for not helping me.*

It was abundantly clear that Satan was indeed my enemy. He not only *wanted* victory in my eating habits, he *had* victory in my eating habits.

Who the Devil Is the Devil?

The world gives a distorted impression of the devil, so it's important for us to know something about Satan and his sphere of influence. Some would have us believe the devil (Satan) is not a real being, and even if he is, they say he doesn't take a personal interest in us as individuals. The Scriptures say Satan (also known in the Bible as the Devil, Lucifer, the evil one, the serpent, son of the morning, and the accuser among other names) is a powerful being, a fallen angel, and the leader of countless demons (other fallen angels) who blinds the world to God's gift of eternal life and seduces believers. Although he is a forceful influence, Satan is *not* omnipresent (everywhere present), omniscient (all knowing), or omnipotent (all powerful). Those attributes are reserved for God.

The Scriptures warn that Satan is cunning and crafty, and those warnings should be taken seriously and literally. To ignore his reality leaves us vulnerable to his deception and attacks. Satan is a terrorist—a patient, cunning terrorist—and he does not follow honorable rules of engagement. His focus is on defeating and discouraging believers, and he will employ any scheme possible, including other people and circumstances. Until we recognize the true enemy, we are jabbing at windmills.

I don't claim to completely understand how Satan operates, nor do I claim to be so important that he personally takes time to attack me, but whether personally or through his demons, Satan deceptively attacks you and me on a daily and individual basis. Yet Satan cannot be directly blamed for things I do wrong, and he is not hiding in my refrigerator or pantry forcing me to eat. In other words, I can't say, *the devil made me do it.* He is sneaky and crafty, but *I* am responsible for my actions.

The Father of Lies

In John 8, Jesus explained to a group of unbelievers why they didn't understand his parables. He said it is because "you belong to your father, the devil, and you want to carry out your father's desire. He was a murderer from the beginning, not holding to the truth, for there is no truth in him. When he lies, he speaks his native language, for *he is a liar and the father of lies*" (John 8:44, emphasis mine).

Satan *is* the father of lies. He *does not* make us lie or make us commit any other sin, but he is a liar and he seeks to mislead the world. As believers, we are responsible to know God's truths so well that we aren't fooled by Satan's deceitfulness. Though he exalts himself above God, the truths in the Bible refute his lies. "For the weapons of our warfare are not carnal but mighty in God for pulling down strongholds, *casting down arguments and every high thing that exalts itself against the knowledge of God…*" (2 Corinthians 10:4-5, emphasis mine).

The Bible says Satan is craftier than any other creature God created (Genesis 3:1);

and there is nothing worse than a crafty liar. What better place to work his lies and deceit than in our eating, something we do every day? Is it any wonder the first sin involved Satan (a liar) and food (fruit), and a tasty food at that?

The lies most difficult to recognize are those shrouded in truth, and Satan is a master of this technique. Note his pattern in Genesis 3:1-13.

The Lie: "...*Did God really say, 'You must not eat from any tree in the garden'?*"
The Truth: God told Adam and Eve not to eat from only *one* tree in the garden, the tree of the knowledge of good and evil, not *all* the trees. Satan used a simple, subtle question about food to divert Eve's focus and plant doubt in her mind.

The Lie: "*You will not surely die," the serpent said to the woman.*"
The Truth: Though Adam and Eve did not experience immediate death, their disobedience caused separation from God (spiritual death) and, ultimately, physical death.

The Lie: "*For God knows that when you eat of it your eyes will be opened....*"
The Truth: Adam and Eve's disobedience *did* open their eyes, *but* they did not have God's divine sight.

The Lie: "...*you will be like God...*"
The Truth: Adam and Eve were created in God's image (Genesis 1:26-27), but Satan appealed to Eve's pride and ego by proposing an exalted position.

The Lie: You'll know "...*good and evil.*"
The Truth: Adam and Eve would see the difference between good and evil, but Satan insinuated they would be on the same level as God, again proposing a loftier position.

Eve allowed her focus to be diverted from obedience to God to self—what *she* could gain; what *she* could be; what *she* could know. The fruit itself was not sinful; rather, it was Eve's disobedience to God's command that was the sin.

Adam and Eve experienced the most intimate human relationship with God that man has ever known. They were created innocent and without sin. They walked and talked with God every day. Then, why didn't they heed his command? Why didn't they run instead of conversing with the enemy? How could they so easily fall into sin? 1 Timothy 2:14 says Eve was *deceived* by the serpent. If this woman, who was daily in God's presence (and without a weight problem), could be deceived by the enemy and enticed with food, how much more will Satan be able to fool you and me?

The New Testament records the account of Satan's temptation of Jesus in the wilderness (Matthew 4:1-11; Mark 1:12-13; Luke 4:1-13). This time Satan was not up against a mere mortal; he was tempting Jesus Christ—God himself.

After he fasted and prayed for forty days in the wilderness, Jesus was naturally weak with hunger. Satan quickly took advantage of the situation and attacked at a physically vulnerable moment. He appealed to Jesus' hunger, attacked his divinity, tested his pride and ego, and tried to seduce him with greed. But, when confronted by the enemy, Jesus answered back with the power of Scripture; he defeated the enemy with the Sword of the Spirit (Ephesians 6:17). Finally, when Jesus had done all that obedience required, God sent angels to minister to him.

These two Biblical accounts show us:

- Satan is deceptive, deceitful, and cunning.
- Satan's deception with Eve was *not about the fruit*; it was about bringing death into the world and destroying the intimacy between God and Adam and Eve.
- The temptation to turn stones into bread was *not about the food*; it was about turning glory and worship away from God to Satan.
- Eve did not resist or run from temptation; instead, she entered into conversation with the enemy.
- If Satan has the audacity to tempt the God of the universe, the King of kings, the Lord of lords, how much more will he try to tempt us?
- From personal experience, Jesus understands the enemy and the temptations we face.
- Satan will use whatever is at hand (even food) to distract and defeat us.
- Satan knows our weaknesses and capitalizes on our vulnerable moments.
- It is vital that we know the Word of God so we can counterattack Satan's lies with God's truth.
- Satan makes empty promises that he can never satisfy.
- When we act in obedience, God will send help.

The Pain of Deceit

A number of years ago I lost a very good friend, not to death but to deceit. My friend was led to believe things about me that weren't true, and eventually those lies destroyed our relationship. The breach was never repaired, and a wonderful friendship was destroyed, leaving an empty spot in my heart.

Can you recall an incident when someone told a lie about you, and you felt helpless to do anything about it? Do you remember the hurt, the anger, and the frustration you felt? When I recognized Satan as my enemy, I felt like blinders were removed from my eyes. I was angry and ready to fight. I realized he had been deceiving me and lying to me for my entire life. I felt I could finally focus on a specific enemy, not the elusive appetite, potluck dinner, chocolate bar, thin friend, or birthday celebration. I realized many of my failures were the result of listening to his subtle deceit.

Lies of the Accuser

For much of my Christian life, I avoided studying Scriptures that pertained to Satan. I was fearful of giving him too much attention and allowing my thoughts to dwell on him. But, I failed to distinguish the difference between *dwelling* on my enemy and being *knowledgeable* about my enemy. Dwelling on him is wrong, but knowing his battle tactics and strategies is intelligent warfare. While the enemy was attacking me with lies and deceit, I was stabbing at windmills!

Not only did I listen to the enemy's lies, I turned those lies into excuses for weight-loss failures. Read the following list and see if you have done likewise. Notice how often the lies are shrouded in truth.

I can't lose weight. I've tried many times, and I always fail. Just the fact you've continued to try again and again proves you're not a failure. A failure is one who falls and refuses to get up just one more time. As you read these pages, you will discover ways to prepare yourself for battle you never thought of before. You will learn why *it's not just about the weight*. Don't stop now; you've just recognized the enemy! You "...can do everything through [Christ] who gives [you] strength..." (Philippians 4:13).

No one supports me. I'm all alone. You are *not* alone! God has promised he will never leave you or forsake you (Hebrews 13:5). In addition to your heavenly help, prayerfully seek and choose a *battle buddy*—someone who will pray *for* you and *with* you, and on whom you can call upon for help and encouragement.

I'm not worthy of God's love. I can't ask him for help. None of us is worthy, *but* he loves you anyway and wants the very best for you. He wants to be the one to help you win your battles. "...Come boldly to the throne of grace, that [you] may obtain mercy and find grace to help in time of need" (Hebrews 4:16).

It's too late for me. I'm too old to lose weight, and my skin will sag. It's never too late to be obedient and start caring for your body. Your skin *may* sag as you lose weight, but don't let that stop you from doing what's right. Fight today's battle today, and quit worrying about what *might* happen tomorrow.

I'll start my diet next week. I'll start after my vacation. I'll start after…. Don't put off obedience. Yes, you can start again, for Jesus loves you, and his arms are always open. However, you may suffer the natural physical consequences of excess weight, and at some point those consequences will become irreversible.

Food makes me feel better. I deserve to eat… Don't settle for second-rate satisfaction. Food is a gift from God for you to enjoy, but food is *not* to replace the fulfillment and satisfaction he longs to give you through himself. Satan will use anything—even food—to keep you from seeking complete contentment in the Lord.

If I'm truly godly (spiritual), I should be able to lose weight. This is one of Satan's most dangerous lies to keep you always questioning your commitment. But you're in good company; even the Apostle Paul struggled to do right (Romans 7:14-20). As you read on, you will discover how you can be well prepared to fight some spiritual battles, yet ill equipped to fight others.

I can't afford to eat healthy food; it's just too expensive. As you consume less food, your grocery bill will shrink, and you'll find fresh fruits and vegetables and meals prepared from scratch are less expensive than prepackaged foods. If you need to adjust your budget, but God will make provision as you are obedient to him (Philippians 4:19).

I must eat all the food on my plate; there are starving children in… Words like these contribute to the development of poor eating habits. Perhaps you grew up hearing this nonsense and were urged to eat every morsel on a plate piled with more food than you needed. Wasting food *is* wrong, but serving too much food is also wrong. Eating it all will not right the wrong.

My metabolism is slow. God must want me to be overweight. God wants you healthy to serve him. Exercise, combined with healthy eating, will speed up your metabolism and help burn fat. If you are eating right and exercising regularly but still not getting results, ask your doctor for help. You may have a correctible metabolic disorder.

I'll cheat just this once. I can make up for it later. You *can* eat less tomorrow, and you *can* exercise later, but *you only have this moment to be obedient for this moment's battle.*

I'll hurt people's feelings if I don't eat what they prepared for me. Unfortunately, that will sometimes be necessary; however, most people will support you when they understand what you're doing. If you feel you absolutely must taste the food, ask for a small portion.

One day I made a homemade cherry pie for my friends Jerri and Steve. Cherry pie was Steve's favorite. I picked the cherries from my own tree, pitted them, and made the crust from scratch. After supper I served the pie, but Steve politely refused, saying he was watching his weight. I tried to coax him into eating a piece as I droned on about how hard I'd worked to prepare the pie just for him. Steve looked me straight in the face and said, "Mary, I'll accept the gift, but not the guilt." I've never forgotten his answer!

It doesn't matter what I look like on the outside; it's only what's in my heart that matters. You were put on earth to minister to people, and your appearance should never be a distraction to that purpose. There's a balance between letting yourself go physically and trying to look like a fashion model. God never intended that his creation should appear slovenly or unkempt.

I must not have been sincere enough when I prayed. Sincere prayer is a vital weapon in your battle, but you must learn to use it effectively. Prayer is not a magic wand or a bargaining tool to get what you want. You can't pray, "Help me lose weight" and expect the fat to fall off your thighs or for your desire for fattening food to instantly diminish. God isn't impressed with the eloquence of your prayers, but with the purity and humility of your heart.

I don't have time to eat healthy and exercise. I'm too busy with work, or kids, or ministry, or... What is more important than maintaining a healthy body to better serve God and others? Just as you set aside time to spend in God's Word to maintain your spiritual health, you need time for exercise and healthy food preparation to maintain your physical health. If you're too busy, reevaluate your time. If you're neglecting your priorities, you have problems beyond overeating.

When I eat in a restaurant, I have to eat everything or I'll be wasting money. God doesn't want you to waste money, so here are three ideas for eating out: order smaller portions from the appetizer section of the menu, share with a friend, or take half your meal home to eat later.

My life is too complicated right now. I'll lose weight when my circumstances improve. What better time to let God work in your life than when you're experiencing problems? He is a big God, bigger than your circumstances. The greater the opposition, the greater the victory.

When I reach my goal weight, I'll be able to eat like everyone else. This is *my* favorite lie. In fact, I believed it so passionately that I gained my weight back every time I lost it. You will *not* be able to eat like everyone else; you need to eat *better* than everyone else. *Battling is for life!*

Examine this list one more time. What is it that each lie has in common? Answer: **It's all about me!** Your thinking and focus have been self-centered, but now they should be changing. You have enlisted in the Lord's army; you are in training, watching out for the enemy, and planning ways to stave off his attacks.

Righteous Indignation

Revelation 12:10 says Satan makes accusations against believers day and night. Can you picture Satan spending countless gleeful hours before God's throne accusing frustrated dieters as they futilely stab at windmills? Does it make you angry? I hope so! If you are genuinely angry with the enemy because he has lied to you, deceived you, and accused you, you are on your way to understanding why winning the battle of the bulge is *not just about the weight*. You are on your way to understanding why you have failed in the past, and why preparation and planning is vital to the victory in your future.

"Finally, be strong in the Lord and in his mighty power. Put on the full armor of God so that you can take your stand against the devil's schemes. For our struggle is not against flesh and blood, but against the rulers, against the authorities, against the powers of this dark world and against the spiritual forces of evil in the heavenly realms" (Ephesians 6:10-12).

Satan Is a Thief

One evening, our family went to a work party at our church. I walked into the sanctuary, laid my purse on the back pew, and went to the rear of the building to clean with the group. A couple of hours later, I gathered my children to leave and reached for my purse. To my dismay, it was considerably lighter. When I looked inside, I realized my leather wallet, a gift from my father, was missing. There had been no money in my wallet, but my diamond earrings, an anniversary gift from my husband, had been in the change compartment. I was devastated at the loss of those gifts.

Earlier in the evening, our daughter Rachel saw a stranger enter the church. Assuming he was looking for her dad, she and her friends went back to playing in another room. We realized the man must have seen my purse on the pew and stolen my wallet.

We called the police, and from Rachel's detailed description, they immediately identified the thief, a drunkard who was notorious for his criminal behavior. But the police couldn't arrest him because no one had witnessed the actual crime. I went home in anger and frustration. I knew who the robber was, but could do nothing about it. During the next two years, I saw the thief on numerous occasions, and each time, my anger was rekindled because of what he had stolen from me.

Satan is a thief who has stolen our time, our joy, and our health. Worst of all, he has stolen the praise, worship, and glory that rightly belong to the Lord. Yes, he is a powerful enemy, but we have a more powerful ally, "…because the one who is in you is greater than the one who is in the world" (1 John 4:4). Our hands are not tied. We can take action. We can "arrest" the thief through the power of the Holy Spirit. We can defeat the thief with the weapons God provides, for he has disarmed the enemy for us (Colossians 2:15).

There is much more to be learned about the strategies and tactics of the enemy, but before we do, let's begin to prepare a battle plan and see why we've failed in the past. Let's find out why, if we learn to obey our commander in chief, our enemy doesn't have a prayer for victory!

Prayer: Dear Lord, Thank you for showing me that my real enemy is Satan—not food, not people, not my appetite, and not my circumstances. Please forgive me for listening to his lies, and forgive me for not acting in obedience. From this moment, I want to feed on your Word, not on Satan's lies. Help me be alert and recognize Satan's deceit and attacks. I want to give you the praise, the worship, and the glory you deserve. In Jesus' name, I pray. Amen.

Memory Verse: *"Be self-controlled and alert. Your enemy the devil prowls around like a roaring lion, looking for someone to devour. Resist him, standing firm in the faith, because you know that your brothers throughout the world are undergoing the same kind of sufferings."* 1 Peter 5:8-9

Food for Thought

Satan is cunning and crafty, and wants you to be defeated.

1. What are some of Satan's lies you have believed?
2. What can you do to resist the enemy?
3. Can you name some things Satan has stolen from you?
4. How are you now more aware of the enemy's tactics?

PLANNING FOR BATTLE

*"Praise be to the LORD my Rock, who trains my
hands for war, my fingers for battle."*
Psalm 144: 1

"You prepare a table before me in the presence of my enemies."
Psalm 23: 5

CHAPTER FIVE

Planning for Battle

For nearly two years, troops, weapons, and vehicles were shipped to England from the United States in preparation for the largest amphibious military attack in the history of the world, an operation that would come to be known as Operation Overlord. Over 150,000 British, American, Canadian, and other Allied troops would join together for battle against Adolph Hitler's forces on the beaches of Normandy, France, D-Day, June 6, 1944.

In December 1943, General Dwight D. Eisenhower was appointed Supreme Allied Commander of the American and European forces and given the awesome responsibility of coordinating all aspects of the invasion. From 1942 on, British intelligence gathered information on the strength and tactics of the enemy in France to ascertain the best location for the assault. Troops were trained on both sides of the Atlantic in preparation for the invasion.

In a matter of days, the Allies were able to push advance into France, and in less than three months the French were liberated. *The planning and preparation had taken longer than the battle.*

We would never have sent our troops into that battle without the proper training, weapons, and battle plans. The casualties would have been even greater than they were, and perhaps, the war would have been lost. Yet many of us try to win battles in our lives with no planning or preparation, and we continue to be frustrated in our defeats.

I knew I would need to plan and prepare if I no longer wanted the temporary changes I'd experienced on commercial diet plans. Diets had given me someone else's plan; now, I wanted to develop a plan for myself based on God's healthy foods and my tastes. I wanted to make permanent changes in the way I ate, and I wanted to establish an exercise program that was realistic for my lifestyle, physical capabilities, and bodily needs. While a specific commercial diet might be right for some people, I no longer wanted to count calories, carbohydrates, or fat grams, and worry whether the foods I needed would be available when we ate away from home.

During our Florida vacation, I began to formulate my strategy and I took the first step by limiting my soda and cutting my portions. It was a good place to start, but when I settled back into my normal routine, I realized I would need a contingency plan for every eating battle if I was to have victory.

The Sunday after we arrived home, I was put to my first test. Our church was having its monthly potluck dinner, and later that afternoon, a lady from our church was celebrating her ninetieth birthday—two battles in one day! At the time, we were living in rural Nebraska, and the food at our church dinners was incredible. Everyone brought out their most delectable dishes, and I was tempted to take a day off from battling. Instead, I formulated a plan that I use to this day—I determined in *advance* what I would eat and the quantity. I decided not to wait to make my choices until I was standing in front of the food. I knew if I waited until I faced the temptation, the battle would be lost.

The evening before, I determined to eat small portions from the healthiest dishes— lean meats, vegetables, fruits, and salads, and *I wouldn't even look at the dessert table, even if a piece of pie called my name!* I didn't know the precise foods that would be served, but from past church dinners, I could make a realistic plan.

Next, I planned and prepared for the birthday party. Again, I didn't know what would be served, but I reasonably assumed there would be cake, nuts, mints, coffee, and punch. I determined to have a glass of punch and some nuts, and then move away from the table. *I wouldn't even look at the cake!*

Do you know what happened? I followed my plan and won the victory in both battles. I concentrated on diligence, self-control, and obedience to the Lord rather than food. I wasn't deprived, and my appetite was satisfied—not gorged as at previous church dinners. I was satisfied! *The planning and preparation had taken longer than the battle.* But do you know when the battle was really won? It wasn't at the serving table when I said no to the larger portions and desserts; it was the evening before when I *prepared my battle plan.*

The idea of planning in advance worked so well that Vikki and I adopted it as our weekly course of action. We kept a daily journal to list upcoming food battles—parties, lunches with friends, church dinners, etc—and predetermined what and how much food we would eat. We recorded our weight losses or gains, our victories and defeats, and insights from our personal devotions. Each Monday we shared our information, committed to pray for each other throughout the week, and had a short Bible study. As battle buddies, accountability to each other and to ourselves through journaling became a vital part of our battle plans.

I've subsequently led numerous battle groups, and invariably those with the greatest weight loss and spiritual growth were those who diligently preplanned, kept a progress journal, and had personal daily devotions.

As I watched some people struggle with the journal concept, I recognized the need for an easy-to-use notebook, and the result was the *Planning for the Battle of the*

Bulge companion workbook/journal. This one-year workbook/journal is designed for individuals or groups. The first twelve weeks offer daily Bible verses and questions that correspond to this book, and Scripture references are provided for the remaining weeks of the year. It includes weight and measurement charts, and there are places to trace your victories and defeats, your weekly objectives, and your character development. You can also record and plan your upcoming battles as well as what foods you will eat for your regular meals.

I review my battle plans each evening before I go to bed, and in the morning, I'm ready to go. I know what and how much I'm going to eat. I have my weapons drawn, and I'm ready for the enemy. When I preplan, I don't spend my in-between mealtimes dwelling on food.

Kim was in the first battle group to use the notebook/journal. She enjoyed our class Bible study and began to lose weight, but she thought the concept of weekly battle planning and having a battle buddy was, in her words, "goofy." After a few weeks, however, she decided to try planning ahead for her battles and writing down all the food she ate. She was amazed at how much food she actually consumed and found that by planning ahead, she had fewer defeats and more victories. Now, after a weight loss of more than seventy pounds, she no longer thinks a battle plan is goofy.

Does it sound like a lot of work? It's easier than you think, and you will have positive results. What if General Eisenhower had decided planning and training for an invasion into France was too much work? The freedom we experience today is a direct result of his planning, preparation, and execution of a battle plan. God wants to give you freedom, too; he wants to work in every area of your life—physical, mental and emotional, and spiritual. He wants to work with you to plan, prepare, and execute a battle plan that is designed with your food tastes, lifestyle, and bodily needs in mind.

Don't underestimate the value of planning and preparing.

Establishing Your Objectives

When the Allies invaded Normandy, their final objective was to permanently liberate all of Nazi-occupied Europe, but that primary goal was divided into smaller attainable goals—taking the coastal beaches of France, pushing the Germans back, and liberating France, among others. Each objective involved specific planning, preparation, and implementation.

For thirty years, my final objective was to be permanently thin—period. I didn't care how I got there, and I didn't care how I stayed there. If I did lose weight, I always gained it back because my "plan" only included picking a diet that promised speedy results, reaching my goal or getting close to it, then eating as I had before I started. I finally realized if I was to reach my ultimate objective (and maintain it), I would have to break the process into smaller goals and patiently realize each one through discipline, diligence, responsibility, honesty, endurance, and more, none of which had been part of any of my previous plans.

I laid out my objectives and divided the planning and preparation into three categories: physical, mental and emotional, and spiritual. My fad diets had focused primarily on the physical aspect. Other diets had combined the physical with the mental and emotional, but dismissed the spiritual. Did I ever experience success with either of these methods? Yes! But we are not just physical beings with emotions; we are also the spiritual creations of a personal God. Our physical being, our mental and emotional being, and our spiritual being are separate, yet we are *one* being, made up of all three parts. We need to plan, prepare, and execute in all three areas to meet our objectives, for each of those areas dramatically affects the other two.

I had tried the purely physical approach by simply dieting until I became bored, frustrated, or hungry. I had tried the physical *with* the mental and emotional approach: picked a diet, gritted my teeth, and told myself that *this time I would succeed because I was worth it*. And, I had tried adding the spiritual element through prayer and Bible study. But I never had had a plan that prepared me in all three areas of my life *before* I went into battle.

To be a victorious soldier, you must be balanced in all three categories. To sustain your physical health and be productive at home, at work, in the community, and at church, you must eat healthy food and get plenty of rest and exercise. To sustain your mental and emotional health, you must guard your mind from negative influences and develop positive, supportive relationships with other believers. To sustain your spiritual health and utilize God's armor and weapons, you must spend time daily in prayer and reading the Scriptures.

Now, please understand, I am *not* saying you must have your whole life in order before you begin to lose weight. I'm saying you need to determine your goals and objectives and develop a plan that encompasses all three areas of your life. Then, *as you execute your plan*, you *are* developing godly character, you *are* transforming your emotional and mental outlook, you *are* experiencing more physical energy and better health, and you *are* steadily losing weight. You can see—*it's not just about the weight*!

Tips for Establishing and Executing Your Battle Plan

Genesis 27 records an account of Jacob and his brother Esau. One day Esau was coming home from an unsuccessful hunting trip and was enormously hungry. He came across his younger brother Jacob cooking stew and asked for a bowl of food. Cunningly, Jacob refused, but offered to sell it to him for the birthright to which Esau was entitled as the older brother. You know the rest—Esau sold the birthright to Jacob and regretted it forever.

But consider some thoughts about this story. Why, as an experienced hunter, didn't Esau *plan* and *prepare* for the possibility that he might not make a kill? Why didn't he take extra food along for the hunting trip? Esau's failure to plan and prepare cost him his birthright, caused family division, and ultimately world tension over the division between Israel and the Arab nations.

Your lack of planning and preparation may not have worldwide consequences, but you can avoid some pitfalls. Here are some guidelines to help you plan for your battle *physically, mentally and emotionally, and spiritually*. Notice how many of these points fall into all three categories.

Physical Battle Planning

- Begin with a thorough medical examination. Don't put yourself through the potential frustration of not being able to lose weight because of a treatable medical issue. If you have faithfully adhered to a healthy eating and exercise plan and have not lost weight, consult your doctor for any special tests you may need. It may be a problem that can be solved by simply avoiding certain foods. Ask your doctor or a licensed dietician for guidance in preparing a personal eating plan that is right for you.
- Prayerfully determine your weight-loss objective and record it in your journal. Allow a realistic time frame to reach your goal, and write out how you intend to reach it. If you need to lose more than a few pounds, consider dividing your long-range objective into short-term goals of five or ten pounds.
- Don't skip meals. You will be hungrier and more likely to consume an unhealthy snack in between meals or to overeat at your next meal.
- Determine if there are foods you need to restrict or give up entirely.

- Plan for your difficult times of day. Get to know your body; at what time of the day are you hungriest? When you feel like you must have something to eat, be prepared with a healthy snack. Keep fresh fruits and vegetables cut up and washed for quick, easy-to-grab snacks.
- Plan your portion size. If you put too much food on your plate, put it away to eat later or throw it away.
- Don't eat any more than a light snack in the three-hour period before you go to bed. This will give your food time to digest and your body can rest through the night.
- Drink water throughout the day. Keep a glass or bottle of water handy at all times. If you don't like water, add a few drops of lemon juice for flavor. You can develop a taste for it.
- Eat until you're satisfied, not until you're gorged. If you genuinely need more food, you can always get more later. Give yourself a chance to be satisfied.
- Arrange your schedule so you have time for regular exercise.

Mental and Emotional Battle Planning

- Determine the mental and emotional objectives you want to achieve (less stress, contentment, etc) and record them in your journal. Allow a realistic time frame to reach your goals, and write out how you intend to reach your objectives.
- Don't go to war alone. Choose at least one battle buddy (accountability partner) to meet with you on a weekly basis. Share your ideas for preparing battle plans, pray together, and encourage each other. Consider bringing others into your battle circle and forming group accountability.
- Put your weight chart where you can see your progress and your food chart where you can see what you have already eaten.
- Plan for stressful times of the year such as sending the kids off to school, demanding times at work, taxes, holidays, or anniversaries of tragic events (death of a loved one, etc). Eating will not relieve the stress or solve the problem.
- Prepare for stressful situations—exams, job interviews, major life decisions, etc. If you overeat when you are stressed, you have not developed a satisfactory

method of dealing with the situation and people involved. Stress should initiate your awareness to face your problems with God's help (1 Peter 4:19).

- Don't linger at the cupboard or refrigerator, and don't peruse the restaurant menu. Consider your options *before* you walk into the kitchen or restaurant and determine what you will eat.

- Eating battles can be triggered by emotions—disappointment, anger, loneliness, joy, a woman's monthly cycle, and more. If you typically overeat during those times, each time you experience that emotion, your body and mind will crave food. Retrain your mind to respond to negative emotional situations. *Battles begin in the mind; battles are won in the mind.*

- Battles may begin in the mind, but they can also be triggered by the senses— smell, sight, hunger, taste, and hearing. Create a plan for those times of temptation.

- Remember the satisfied feeling you have when you win a victory. Train your mind and body to crave that feeling again.

- Make a grocery list and *stick with it.* Don't give into impulse shopping, and don't shop when you're hungry. Make most of your food purchases from the perimeter of the store—fresh fruits and vegetables, fresh cuts of meat, and dairy products. Avoid or limit processed sugar, processed meats, white flour, canned and prepackaged foods, caffeine, artificial sweeteners and additives, and carbonated soft drinks. Don't be unbalanced in any food group. Avoid diets that exclude certain food groups and lean heavily on one or two others.

Spiritual Battle Planning

- Determine the spiritual objectives you want to achieve (discipline, joy, diligence, etc) and record them in your journal. Allow a realistic time frame to reach your goals, and write out how you intend to reach your objectives.

- Begin your day with prayer and personal devotions. When Jesus was tempted by Satan in the wilderness, he responded with Scripture. If morning is not good for you, determine the best time and make it a regular part of each day. It will provide strength and direction.

- Develop a Scripture memorization program. At the end of each chapter, I've provided a suggested memory verse that will give you courage and strength throughout the day. You may want to write out the verse on a three-by-five-inch card and carry it with you.
- At the beginning of each week, prepare a battle plan for the next six days. Each evening before you go to bed, review your plan for the following day.
- Review and evaluate your battles at the end of each day—why did you experience victory or defeat; what emotions were you feeling; did you pray; did you charge the enemy? Use that time to change what *did not* work and refine what *did* work. Praise God for your victories, and acknowledge your defeats.
- When you step up to the buffet line, open the refrigerator, or consult a menu, ask yourself how you can build godly character in the situation. Your focus will be brought back to Christ and your character development. It will remind you who your enemy is and strengthen your resolve to defeat him.
- Sing praises, hymns, and other uplifting songs throughout the day.
- Claim promises from God's Word.
- Ask yourself these questions when you are faced with a food battle:
    1. Have I prayed?
    2. Am I hungry, or am I actually thirsty?
    3. Should I exercise instead of eat?
    4. Am I eating because of my emotions? If so, what is bothering me, and how should I deal with the problem?
    5. Who is the enemy and what does he want to accomplish in my life right now?
    6. What does God want to accomplish in my life right now?
    7. What is my battle really about and what are my long-term goals?
    8. Am I deceiving myself in any way?
    9. Will eating _____ be harmful to my health?
    10. Do I now choose God's gift of healthy food in reasonable portions or Satan's counterfeit?

Neglect It No Longer

David's amazing triumph over the giant Goliath (1 Samuel 17) brought victory for Israel and glory to the Lord. But I don't think the most significant part of the conquest came when Goliath hit the dirt. I believe David's real victory was in his years of obedience to his father while he tended the family's sheep, while he played his harp and wrote songs of praise to the Lord, and while he spent endless hours practicing with his slingshot in preparation to protect the flock. When David stood before Goliath, I don't think he had any doubt that the stone would hit its mark. David was *prepared* spiritually, emotionally, mentally, and physically, and when faced with a foe, he executed his *plan* without hesitation.

Perhaps you are a Christian who has had great victories in some areas of your life, but your weight is a battle that you just can't seem to win. You have spent years building a solid foundation in Christ and you have put on the armor of God (Ephesians 6), yet victory over your appetite and weight eludes you. Could it be that you have been so busy fighting other battles that this one has been neglected? *Neglect it no longer.* Get out your slingshot, pick up your stones, and develop and prepare a battle plan that will work for you. As you go to war, apply those same weapons to your battle of the bulge that you have effectively used to win other battles.

Preparing the plan that is right for you will take time and work, and you will have to make adjustments along the way. You are fortunate to live in a day and age in which you have a multitude of resources available to you—doctors, dieticians, health and exercise books and videos, the Internet, health clubs, and more. Just as you attend retreats, seminars, and conferences and read books and magazines for family, job, and ministry enhancement, use those resources to plan and prepare for better health.

Caught Off Guard

Believing the enemy had left the area, the American soldiers explored the deserted German campsite. They felt safe—at least as safe as one could feel in war-torn Europe in the 1940s. Then they heard voices—*speaking German!* The Americans had to make a swift decision. Gunfire might draw more of the enemy, and they didn't know how many were in the vicinity. If they ran back to their own camp, they would reveal the location of the entire division, that is, if they made it back to camp. Fearful that any movement would draw the enemy's attention, they silently stole toward a partially hidden trench they had seen beyond the campsite. With no time to spare, they jumped the hedge, rolled into the trench, and lay flat as the Germans came closer. Within seconds, the Americans realized what their hiding place was—an old enemy latrine. But there was nothing they could do; to move could mean possible death. The choice was made for them—stay in the filth and clean up the mess later. My father, Lieutenant Philip J. Englund, and his fellow soldiers had been caught off guard.

There will be times when you will be caught off guard despite your best efforts at planning and preparation. It would be nice to think you will never suffer defeats or lose ground to the enemy, but that's not reality. Some days you will charge the enemy and advance further than you hoped, while other days you'll feel like you're right back in boot camp. There will be times when you feel fortunate to simply hold the enemy at bay, and other times you will lie in the muck and wait for discouragement and the enemy to pass.

But *don't quit*! Cry out to your faithful God, and he will raise you up and clean away the mess.

"I waited patiently for the LORD; he turned to me and heard my cry. *He lifted me out of the slimy pit*, out of the mud and mire, he *set my feet on a rock*, and gave me a firm place to stand. He put a new song in my mouth, a hymn of *praise to our God*" (Psalm 40:1-3, emphasis mine).

Prayer: Dear Lord, help me as I plan, prepare, and execute a healthy eating plan for my battle of the bulge. Thank you for reminding me there is no middle ground in battle; either I will fulfill the plan you have for me, or I will fulfill no plan, which is what Satan wants for me instead. Thank you for bringing me out of the mire and setting me on the Rock. In Jesus' name, I pray. Amen.

Memory Verses: *"Blessed be to the LORD my Rock, who trains my hands for war, my fingers for battle." Psalm 144: 1*
"He prepares a table before me in the presence of my enemies." Psalm 23: 5

Food for Thought

Using "Tips for Establishing and Executing Your Battle Plan," write out your objectives and goals, how you will prepare yourself for battle, and how you will execute your battle plan. Check your objectives and goals frequently and record your progress, and remember to be flexible as they will probably evolve over the course of your war.

CHAPTER SIX

UNDERSTANDING
WHY YOU FAIL

*"I would have lost heart, unless I had believed that I would
see the goodness of the LORD in the land of the living.
Wait on the LORD; Be of good courage, and He shall
strengthen your heart; Wait, I say, on the LORD."*
Psalm 27:13-14

CHAPTER SIX

Understanding Why You Fail

"I don't want to hurt your feelings, but why would anyone want to buy a book written by you? No one knows your name, you didn't lose a hundred and fifty pounds, and you don't have a Ph.D. You're just not qualified, and the market is flooded with books like yours."

With high hopes, I was attending my first writers conference, and I was now nervously seated at a narrow conference table opposite a beautiful, trim book editor. I had just presented my thirty-second pitch for this book, and in less than ten seconds, I went from *fledgling* author to *failed* author. I was devastated.

I stood, thanked her for her time, and shuffled toward the door in a daze. I returned to the remaining workshops, but my mind replayed that conversation throughout the remainder of the day. *That editor is right*, I thought. *No one knows who I am, I'm not qualified, and I can't write. What was I thinking? Why did I spend money I can't afford on this stupid conference? Why didn't I just stay home and do something I'm good at? I'm a failure at this writing stuff, and I haven't even started!"*

The years I spent nursing negative thoughts about my dieting failures primed me to transfer that same destructive thinking to my writing. Does that sound familiar to you? Do you feel like a failure when it comes to dieting? Has someone made disparaging remarks about your weight or physical appearance? Have you been told you're a failure? You may have more dieting disasters than you can count, but don't surrender. You're not a failure; if you were, you wouldn't be reading this book. By the end of this chapter, you will understand why, though you've failed in the past, there is victory in your future.

Why Most Diets Don't Work

Most diets are designed for failure. Now, before you protest, let me explain. Every diet plan on the market, balanced or otherwise, will give you results. But why then, if diets are designed for success, do most people gain back their weight and then some? I believe the answer is that although diets help you take off the weight, most of them don't give you the tools to change your long-term eating behavior and patterns. If you happen to reach your goal weight through sheer determination, then what do you do? What has permanently changed in your thinking and behavior that will help you keep the weight off? What foods will you eat when you return to "real" life?

Failed, But Not a Failure

No war consists only of victories. That's not pessimism; it is reality. But suffering defeats can actually be positive, for defeats reveal our weaknesses and show us where we need further growth and development. Successful leaders study defeats, determine what went wrong, and plan new strategies for the next battle. They don't say, "Gee, I lost a battle today, so I guess I'll give up and forget about the war." That attitude reveals the difference between battling for life and engaging in short-term combat. When you acknowledge that you are in a lifetime war, you will build character, learn to eat right, and *keep the weight off.* When you enter into an occasional skirmish (diet), you may lose some weight, but you will probably gain it back.

God has not designed you for defeat; *he has designed you for victory.* Therefore, understanding why you failed in the past is vital to your future success. You are only a failure if you fall down and refuse to get up and try again! So, rather than being *humiliated* by defeat, we should *humbly* plan and prepare for future battles.

Discouragement is the simple answer for defeat and probably the biggest factor in giving up on a diet. Dieters become discouraged, so they fail; they fail, so they become discouraged. Is that where you are? To stop the cycle you must learn from past mistakes and correct your thinking and behavior.

While keeping our battle theme in mind, let's examine a few of the most common reasons people fail at dieting.

Failure to adequately plan and prepare. Perhaps you've heard the adage *people don't plan to fail, they fail to plan.* This is particularly true when it comes to dieting. When is the last time you consulted your doctor, chose a healthy eating plan (one with servings from all the food groups), determined the character you lacked in adhering to your plan (patience, diligence, discipline, self-control, etc), and determined to develop those character qualities *before* you began?

Until a few years ago, my answer to that question was *never.* My weight-loss pattern went something like this: get totally disgusted with myself, pick a quick weight-loss program from my vast repertoire of fad diets, announce the commencement of my new diet to my friends and family, follow it (more or less) for a few days, and quit. If I lost weight, I told everyone how well I'd done. If I didn't lose weight, I told everyone there must be something wrong with my metabolism, my thyroid must be out of whack, or the diet was stupid!

Once, in my early twenties, I asked my doctor for help to lose weight. I was bitterly disappointed when, instead of a prescription for diet pills, he handed me a brochure that actually required me to record my food intake, exercise regularly, and limit myself to 1,200 calories of healthy food per day. He explained that if I followed the brochure's guidelines I would lose one to two pounds each week. *One to two pounds a week! What was he thinking?* I wanted to ask if he had any idea how long it would take me to reach my goal weight at that snail's pace. I took the brochure home, glanced through it, and tossed it in the trash. Only once in thirty years of dieting did I actually start on the right path by consulting my doctor, and when he gave me good advice, I threw it away.

Military boot camp takes up to twelve weeks for good reason: it takes that long to change habits, redirect thinking, and prepare recruits for warfare. Victorious soldiers will learn obedience to their commanders, be trained to use their weapons, study the enemy, set short-term and long-term goals, prepare for surprise attacks, and develop a oneness with their comrades.

Planning for your battle of the bulge is no different. You don't need to wait twelve weeks to begin to fight your battle. Start today! But you must understand that you will continue to be in training each day and that your primary goal is to permanently change how you think and behave regarding your eating habits. *Preparation* for battle takes as much commitment as actually *fighting* the battle. Don't quit! The training is worth the results.

Lack of patience. We are a society that wants results, and we want them *now!* With that mentality, I have bought countless magazines and tabloids at checkout stands because the headlines read something like: "*Lose 7 to 10 Pounds in One Week*"; "*Get Your Body Ready for the Beach in Eight Short Weeks*"; and, my personal favorite, "*Eat Whatever You Want and Still Lose Weight.*" Usually, I got no further than reading the article, because those diets weren't providing the easy formula I wanted. If I did attempt one of those programs, I didn't stick with it because I didn't get dramatic results. I wanted a quick, painless fix.

Fad diets simply don't offer a realistic plan you can maintain for the rest of your life. Many are not healthy and balanced and are designed with an emphasis on only one or two food groups. Lack of variety will soon become boring, and you will revert to the old habits that gave you temporary emotional and physical satisfaction. Before long, the pounds will be back. Quick fixes don't last in dieting any more than they do in marriages, automobiles, or plumbing!

Most people don't enjoy waiting, but some people have the character to wait. They are not impulsive and take time to make wise decisions. Patience involves time and waiting for the results while working toward a goal. Patience and perseverance go hand in hand.

"*Count it pure joy, my brothers, whenever you face trials of many kinds, because you know that the testing of your faith develops perseverance. Perseverance must finish its work so that you may be mature and complete, not lacking anything*" (James 1: 2-4).

Dieting has always been a testing time for me, *not* pure joy. Because my focus was on immediate results, I remained frustrated, and eventually I gave up. But, according to James, if my focus is on faith and perseverance, there's reward at the end of the test.

Fear of failure. Remember when you were chosen for sports teams at recess in elementary school? Regardless of your personal abilities, you wanted to be picked by the team with the highest skill level; you wanted to be on the winning side. If you were chosen by the team with the biggest and strongest kids, you had no fear of losing because you already knew the outcome. You don't need to fear the outcome of this battle either. *You are on the winning side!*

"...God has not given us a spirit of fear, but of power and of love and of a sound mind" *(2 Timothy 1:7). Because fear does not find its source in God, we know it comes from Satan—an enemy who wants to keep you fearful and defeated before you place one foot onto the battlefield. God wants you to be victorious and will give you power, love, and a sound mind! The choice is yours; you get to choose your own team.*

Fear also comes from lack of preparation and not having a well-developed plan. Without a plan, you don't know where you're going, what or who you are fighting against, or who is on your side. You begin to question your motives, abilities, character, and past failures. You tell yourself you can't win this war because you've failed too many times in the past. But Psalm 56:3 says, "When I am afraid, I will trust in you." You have nothing to fear when your trust is in God. As you begin to understand your enemy and put together a battle plan, you will gain confidence.

Fighting too many battles at one time. We all have multiple battles in our lives—some minor and some major. My weight problem was so consuming that it fell into the major category, and I realized that preparing, planning, and battling would take a lot of time and commitment on my part. But as I began to see the possibilities through developing the battle theme, I wanted to immediately start applying the principles to every area of my life. Though my intentions were good, I realized it wasn't feasible to tackle all my battles at once. If possible, concentrate on one major issue at a time. If your weight is more than you can handle right now, start by eating smaller portions and healthier food, then come back in a few weeks and structure a plan that is right for you. You will have plenty of opportunities to apply your newly developed character later.

Eight months after Vikki and I began meeting together, she and her husband Ken went through a professional devastation that lasted several months. Bill and I prayed, cried, and counseled with them. Both Vikki and Ken told me separately that she made it through that difficult time by utilizing the character she developed while battling her weight. She was prepared to fight the professional battle because she had learned that *battling isn't just about the weight.*

Difficulty. Eating poorly is easy, but planning and preparing takes time, and it *is* hard. That's why you're now viewing your weight loss as a war. Remember, this is a lifetime war made up of daily, sometimes even hourly, battles.

Focus on godly character development, new insights into Scripture, healthy food preparation, a regular exercise program, and, yes, even the pounds you shed as you emerge victorious in battle. You will experience occasional setbacks, but with each victory you will gain strength and courage. "…Be strong and courageous. Do not be terrified; do not be discouraged, for the LORD your God will be with you wherever you go" (Joshua 1:9).

Poor self-image and/or faulty perceptions. Self-perception will directly affect how you face your battles. Do you see yourself as a victorious warrior or a defeated prisoner of war? Are you viewing yourself through the eyes of a God who loves and values you or through the eyes of others and past disappointments?

When I was nine years old, I moved with my mother, stepfather, and two stepbrothers to the Florida Keys from Minneapolis, Minnesota. My parents were divorced and both had recently remarried, and I was starting my fourth new school in five years. On top of that, I was a bit chubby. Needless to say, I had developed a few insecurities. My weight didn't bother me too much until a boy in our new neighborhood began to call me *pig*. Other kids picked it up, and I can still remember my face turning crimson and the embarrassment I felt when someone said, "Hey, pig!" It was devastating. *I'm fat*, I thought, *fat and ugly. Everybody thinks I'm fat and ugly, and nobody likes me.* Throughout my teen years, even when I managed to lose a few pounds, I viewed myself as a *fat pig*.

As I look at old pictures, I see what a faulty perception I had. Yes, I wore a size or two larger than most of the other girls, but I wasn't ugly, fat, or a pig. What I needed was for someone to lovingly show me that while a clean, neat appearance is important, my true value is in the way God views me. I needed someone to show me the wrong foods I was eating and to encourage me to drink water rather than soda and to exercise more. A mentor like that would have saved me years of heartache.

It's sometimes still a struggle for me to see myself through God's eyes, but I have a choice, and so do you. You can either wallow in self-pity or start working toward keeping your body at a healthy weight. You don't have to remain a prisoner of past defeats and failures. Nothing would please Satan more than for you to spend your time and energy berating yourself while living in self-pity, doubt, and failure instead of in obedience and victory.

If you are having difficulty viewing yourself spiritually, emotionally, or physically from God's perspective, seek the counsel of your pastor or a close friend who can help you gain a true viewpoint from the Scriptures. You will begin to know your true worth.

Self-deception. You may be able to hide from your friends and family, but *you cannot hide from God.* As you examine the following list, remember who the father of lies is.

Have you ever done any of the following?

- You lean to the side of the scale that displays your lowest weight.
- You wear your belt below your waistline to wear a smaller pant size.
- You buy high-priced clothing because the size numbers on the labels are smaller.
- You promise yourself you will start your diet tomorrow, or Monday, or after the holidays.
- You won't let anyone take your picture or if you do, you hide on the back row.
- You avoid any situation where you have to give an indication of your clothing size.
- You hide candy wrappers.
- You check out merchandise with a cashier of the same sex so a cashier of the opposite sex won't see what size you wear.
- You wear lightweight clothing to the doctor's office to weigh less on the scale.
- You hide food from other members of your family.
- You hide food from *yourself!*
- You won't look into a full-length mirror.
- Your New Year's resolutions always include unfulfilled commitments about diet and exercise.
- You *lie* about your weight on your driver's license. (Who is the father of lies? Hmm!)
- You cut the tags out of your clothes so no one will know what size you wear.
- You tell people you don't understand why you weigh so much, but you never keep track of all the food you consume, including nibbling and snacking and the condiments you add to your food.
- You drink coffee, tea, soda, and other beverages in place of water.
- You use appetite suppressants instead of self-control.
- You wear clothes that will suppress or conceal the fat to make yourself appear slimmer.
- You drink diet soda with your French fries and dessert.

- You are hiding an eating disorder from your family.
- You are considering major surgery to lose weight so you won't have to use self-control, and you think you will then be able to eat anything you want with no limits. (Are you seriously considering potentially life-threatening surgery? Do you realize that after weight-loss surgery you must limit your portion size and the kinds of food you eat? Do you realize you will essentially be starting a new *diet? You will be starting a new diet, while trying to avoid dieting?*)

Unrealistic expectations. How much weight do you want to lose? What do you expect to look like when you reach your goal weight? Are you the mother of three trying to regain your high school figure? Are you a dad trying to juggle family, career, and church activities but desiring to look like Mr. Universe? Are you a high school or college student who would be at a healthy weight if you lost twenty-five pounds, but you want to lose thirty-five pounds to be ultra thin? Are your expectations realistic?

There's nothing wrong with wanting to look attractive; in fact, you *should* take care of your body and want to look your best. But be cautious of your motives, comparing yourself with others, and setting goals that are unrealistic.

The wrong weapons. What weapons are you using to fight your battle of the bulge—guilt, frustration, unrealistic goals, diet pills, or expensive exercise equipment? How about empty promises to yourself or loved ones? Are you trying each new fad diet that comes on the market? Weapons like those may work for a while, but in the long run they are weak, ineffective, and temporary.

I knew that prayer and Bible study were my obvious spiritual weapons. But while I knew how to use them effectively in other areas of my life, I didn't know how to apply them to my weight battle. I felt like a failure as a Christian. Was I ineffectual in my prayer life? Was I reading the wrong verses in my Bible? No, I just needed more training and preparation. Prayer and Bible study are still at the top of my list, but I am learning that God has many more weapons available for me, and I'm now using them against the right enemy. In Chapter Nine, you will discover an arsenal of weapons and how to use them.

Food as a reward. I can't tell you how many times I've faithfully adhered to a diet and actually lost weight, only to be derailed by rewarding myself with a hot fudge sundae or a high calorie meal at a restaurant. The next day I would step onto the scale and be right back where I started. I was using the very thing I was trying to limit as a reward!

Reward motivation can be good as long as you are using the right reward. God uses it in the Bible, we use it at home with our children, and teachers use it at school. Many businesses use rewards as incentives for their employees to reach higher goals. In the next chapter, we'll examine right and wrong motives and put rewards into perspective.

Focus on self. One of the quickest paths to failure in any battle is to place focus on self. We want to do it *our* way and at our pace. *We* want to be in charge. *We* want others to support and encourage *us*. *We* want people to notice how much weight *we've* lost. *We* want to achieve a certain look or a specific size. *We want...*

You are in the shape you're in because *you* have been the focus and *you* have lived and eaten the way *you* want. Your eating behavior has been totally centered on *you*!

When I started to apply Biblical principles to my weight, it was the first time my efforts were not about *me*. It was the first time I was not focused on how fast *I* could lose, how much *I* could eat, what size *I* would be, and how good *I* could look. Those things have taken care of themselves and have become a natural byproduct of daily obedience and character growth. My focus is finally where it should have been all along—on obedience to God and his will for what I eat.

Emotional overeating. This is nothing more than placing blame on our circumstances and/or other people. It's not a *reason* for failure; it's an *excuse*. Life hasn't gone the way we wanted or expected; therefore, we eat to make ourselves feel better. There is emptiness in our soul that we are trying to fill with food. The problem is that food fills that hole for only a moment and then it's empty again. Christ is the only one who can satisfy our souls.

Emotional eating is a temporary solution, at best, and will nearly always backfire with the negative result of added pounds. Eating when you're angry will *not* resolve conflict or make you feel better about yourself. Eating when you're disappointed will *not* change your circumstances nor get you what you want. Eating will *not* give you friends if you're lonely or restore a broken relationship with a loved one. Eating will *not* make you happy if you are sad and will *not* hurt another person if you are seeking revenge.

Although research shows that certain foods can give comfort from stress, that reprieve is only temporary. Anger, disappointment, loneliness, and other emotions are legitimate issues with which you must deal, but they are problems that cannot be solved with food.

Placing yourself behind enemy lines. During my battle process, I found there were places, times, and situations where I could not be if I wanted to experience victory. It was like placing myself behind enemy lines. I avoided gatherings where the entire focus of the event was on food and eating. I avoided making chocolate chip cookies because I love to eat the dough. The temptations were too great. I learned what I could handle and what I couldn't, and I didn't place myself in situations where defeat was virtually guaranteed.

In 2 Samuel 11, King David was to lead his army into battle, but decided to stay home, sending his generals in his stead. One evening, while strolling on his roof, he looked across to a neighboring rooftop and saw beautiful Bathsheba bathing. Bathsheba was married to Uriah, one of David's soldiers who was away at war. Though David was also married, he gave into his selfish lust, slept with Bathsheba, and she became pregnant. David sent for Uriah in hopes he would sleep with his wife and that David could pass off the child as Uriah's. But, loyal, faithful Uriah refused to rest in his own home while his fellow soldiers were still on the battlefield. David "solved" the problem by having Uriah sent to the battlefront where, according to David's plan, Uriah was killed. David married Bathsheba, but their baby boy died soon after birth. So, David committed adultery, devastated two families, lost his credibility, and two innocent people died, all because he was not where he should have been. *David removed himself from God's protection and placed himself behind the enemy's line.*

Determine what circumstances, social gatherings, times of day, and even which people affect your battle adversely. You will find greater victory when you avoid those situations and people. As you develop self-control and wise eating habits, you will find you can attend those functions again.

Medical problems. I cannot stress enough the importance of getting a medical examination by your physician *before you begin any new eating program*. Not only is it important to have regular checkups, but if you have unsuccessfully attempted to lose weight on a healthy eating plan, you may have a medical problem that your doctor can diagnose.

Kim diligently dieted and exercised for months to lose weight for her son's upcoming wedding and succeeded in *gaining* three pounds. When I met Kim she was understandably frustrated, but was excited about joining our battle group; she felt it might be the answer she was seeking. On the first day of our class, she went to her doctor and discovered she was suffering from a metabolic disorder. Kim followed her doctor's instructions, began to follow the principles in this book, and lost a remarkable thirty-five pounds in the first two months.

Bad habits. When you begin to work on discipline and diligence, you will become aware of how many poor eating habits you have developed.

- *Mindless or boredom eating*—Have you ever been reading a book, watching television, or conversing with a friend when suddenly you realize you've consumed an entire plate of cookies or devoured a whole bag of chips? That's mindless eating—eating without thinking about what or how much you are putting in your mouth. Mindless eating occurs when you don't have a plan.
- *Nibbling while preparing meals*—Keep track of how much food you put in your mouth the next time you are preparing a meal. I have often eaten so much while cooking a meal I wasn't even hungry when I sat down to eat, yet still

proceeded to eat my normal portion at the table. It was like eating two meals in one sitting!

- *Eating out*—When I was a young girl, it was a rare treat for our family to eat in a restaurant. That is no longer the case. Families eat on the run finding it easier to pull into a drive-through window and eat from a bag rather than take time to prepare a healthy meal. While many restaurants are providing healthier options, too many times we "treat" ourselves to the high calorie, fatty choices.

- *Portion control*— Fast-food restaurants now make portions extra large, and instead of taking the extra food home for another meal, we clean our plate of every last morsel. At home we heap our plates with more food than we need, and continue eating after we're full.

- *Late-night eating* —Most doctors agree it is best to eat nothing, or simply a light snack, during the last three hours before bedtime. Even your digestive system needs a rest.

The Choice Is Yours

Can you identify with one or more of the above reasons for dieting failure? Perhaps you could even add to the list. We all have our reasons (excuses), but now you have a choice to make. Will you continue to hide behind your excuses, or will you learn from past failures, prepare for battle, take up your weapons, and go on to victory?

Remember the editor I told you about—the one who said no one would want to read a book by me? I gathered my courage and, with fear and trepidation, approached another editor the following day and presented my pitch. Dan put me at ease and shocked me by saying he believed in what I was writing. He encouraged me to keep going, asked to see my proposal, and gave me a goal for which to strive. I had a choice to make, and the choice I made was to get up and keep trying. I didn't give up, and now, *you are reading this book*!

Prayer: Dear Lord, Thank you for showing me the areas in my life where I have been weak and made excuses. I confess I have failed in the past, but I am not going to remain a failure. I'm going to get up and try again. I know I will sometimes experience defeats in the future, but *I will not give up*. I will arm myself in your strength and will defeat my enemies in your power. In Jesus' name, I pray, Amen.

Memory Verse: *"I would have lost heart, unless I had believed that I would see the goodness of the LORD in the land of the living. Wait on the LORD; be of good courage, and he shall strengthen your heart; wait, I say, on the LORD." Psalm 27:13-14*

Food for Thought

1. Which reasons for failure can you relate to and why?
2. What poor eating habits have you developed that have contributed to failure?
3. In what ways have you been deceiving yourself and others?
4. What new choices are you going to make?**5.**

MOTIVES AND GOALS

"Brethren, I do not count myself to have apprehended; but one
thing I do, forgetting those things which are behind and reaching
forward to those things which are ahead. I press toward the
goal for the prize of the upward call of God in Christ Jesus."
Philippians 3:13-14

Chapter Seven

Motives and Goals

December 12—*Dear Diary, Rachel will be getting married six months from today, and I really need to lose some weight before the wedding. I want to look good for Rachel, for the family, for me. OK, fine—I want to look good for the photos! As soon as the holidays are over, I'll start my diet.*

December 31—*Dear Diary, I can do this; I'm determined! Five months and thirteen days to go until Rachel gets married, and I hereby resolve to lose twenty-five pounds. This'll be a snap—only five pounds per month; one and one quarter pounds per week; three ounces per day. Today I tried on that beautiful beaded cream-colored suit I'm going to wear, and, well, the skirt is a little tight. I want to feel comfortable and relaxed at the ceremony and reception, so it's essential I lose this weight. I'll start the New Year with a new me. I'll start my diet tomorrow.*

January 7—*Dear Diary, today is Jonathan's birthday and I'm going to make that incredible chocolate cake from scratch (his favorite). In a few days, when all the cake is gone, I'll start my diet.*

February 12—*Dear Diary, today is Bill's birthday and he wants to go out to dinner to celebrate. The wedding is four months from today. I wonder why the Lord isn't helping me with my diet.*

February 14—*Dear Diary, the annual church Valentine's Day banquet is tonight and the men are doing all the cooking. I can't wait for that cheesecake they always serve (my favorite). I'll start my diet on Monday.*

March 23—*Dear Diary, today is our twenty-seventh wedding anniversary. My, how quickly the years pass. Rachel's wedding, however, is getting closer, so I really need to get serious about this diet. The skirt I'm wearing for the wedding is still snug—OK, really tight. I'll start my diet tomorrow after Bill and I go out for dinner. I wish God would take away my appetite.*

April 12—*Dear Diary, today is my birthday, and I'll be celebrating all week with my friends. They like taking me out for lunch, and I can't refuse, or I might hurt someone's feelings. I'm really starting my diet next week. I mean it! The wedding is two months from today. I've been patiently waiting for God to help me. Where is he? After all, I want to lose this weight for **him**.*

May 5—*Dear Diary, Rachel is graduating from college today. We'll be attending a* *party and then going out for dinner to celebrate. I only have five weeks until the wedding, and my skirt is still tight. If only the Lord would jumpstart me with the flu or something, I know I could lose the rest.*

June 12—*Dear Diary, Rachel's and Bobby's wedding is today. Rachel is beautiful in her dress and Bobby is so handsome in his tux. This is going to be a wonderful day. But, where are those control-top panty hose and that girdle, anyway?*

I'll Lose Weight for Anything

Funny? Not really. What you just read had been my dieting pattern for years; my ineffective approach to my war on weight. It was two more years and I was several pounds heftier before my thinking began to change.

Whatever major social event loomed on the horizon determined my goals (how much weight I wanted to lose) as well as my motives (what I would wear, and what the people there might think about me). My motives and goals fluctuated in direct accordance to my circumstances.

I've lost weight for family reunions, class reunions, company dinners, graduations, weddings, and funerals. (Funerals are a definite challenge, because you usually only have about three days!) I've lost weight to fit into my old clothes because I couldn't afford a new wardrobe, and because I wanted to look good in a bathing suit during a vacation at the beach. (I *never* reached that goal.) My husband has offered me money and new clothes as incentives, not because he was displeased with me, but because he saw my struggles and frustrations and he was willing to do anything to help.

I've been in groups and lost weight because I was embarrassed not to succeed, and occasionally because they offered a monetary reward to the person who lost the most weight. I've been motivated when people made disparaging comments about my figure, and I've set goals after seeing a particularly beautiful model or movie star on television or in a magazine. I've tried to lose weight to have better health and more energy. I've tried to spiritualize my motives by losing weight to please God, going so far as to make unrealistic promises hoping that would make me feel guilty enough to stay on a diet. I could continue, but by now you get the picture, and perhaps, you can relate.

All—OK, *most*—OK, *some*—of my motives and goals were fairly reasonable, and they usually worked—for a few days, anyway. But events come and go, and when the affair passed, my weight slowly crept back.

The approval of my husband and children was not a strong enough motive for me to maintain a diet. I knew they were going to love me no matter what I looked like—they *had* to love me. And, though my constant dieting exasperated them, they were always supportive.

Other people in my life have not been as generous with their affections and comments. While their remarks usually hurt my feelings, and I adopted an attitude of *I'll show them I can be thin*, I eventually dismissed them as shallow and unworthy of my hard work, and I continued to eat.

As I approached middle age, I tried to motivate myself to exercise regularly with threats of bone loss and sagging skin. The knowledge of increased health risks such as cancer, heart disease, and diabetes did nothing to curb my appetite, and I pushed those potential issues into the future.

My yo-yo dieting, changing goals, and selfish motives only managed to place me in a state of continuous guilt. I felt guilty because I let down my husband, my kids, and my friends. I felt guilty that I had let down God because I promised him I would lose weight and didn't do it and I wasn't taking care of the body he gave me. I felt guilty because I lacked the character to stick with a diet, and because I couldn't keep the weight off when I did lose it. I spent years of wasted time and energy on guilty *could haves* and *should haves*.

The Guilt Trap

Years ago, my friend Susan gave me one of my all-time favorite coffee mugs. She gave me this particular mug because, as a fellow professional dieter, she knew we both carried loads of dieting guilt. The mug pictured an elephant drinking coffee and musing, *Does guilt burn up many calories?* That saying serves as a reminder for me to avoid falling back into the guilt trap.

Many people come to our battle groups carrying a burden of guilt, and it's often the result of failing to live up to the real or imagined unrealistic expectations placed on them by authority figures or family members. Sometimes they have had parents, teachers, and even ministers use guilt to try to pressure them into certain behavior. As guilt-ridden dieters, they are then primed to transfer guilt to their failed dieting attempts.

I believe healthy guilt can be a positive deterrent of wrong behavior and can direct us to make positive changes. But too often we fall into the snare of unhealthy guilt. The difference between the two is discerned by identifying the Biblical conduct *God* requires of us, not what *individuals* demand. Healthy guilt occurs when we realize we've violated a moral or ethical principle or law set down by God. False, or unhealthy, guilt results when we take responsibility for acts we did not commit or when we violate the erroneous standards or expectations of others.

False guilt can also result from breaking irrational or unrealistic vows and commitments we've made to ourselves, others, or God. I once led a weight-loss group in our church based on a then-popular Christian diet book. The author asked the reader to make a lifelong commitment to abstain from all desserts. Wanting to be the heroic, godly leader, I stood before the group and told them and God that neither cheesecake nor chocolate would ever pass my lips again.

I knew the moment I uttered those words that I was making a promise I couldn't (wouldn't) keep, but I hoped by simply making a commitment to God (even one that was unrealistic), I would be motivated to stay true and faithful to my diet. It didn't work, of course, and I felt guilty. Eventually I asked God to forgive me for making such a foolish promise. A realistic commitment, one I could live with, would have been to cut back on the frequency and portion size of my desserts.

I learned my lesson. When I felt the Lord prompting me to curb my soda intake, I determined to cut back to one per week. I knew I would avoid needless guilt by making a commitment that was *reasonable* and *realistic*. Now, on rare occasions, I drink more than one soda per week, but often weeks, even months pass and I drink none. Frankly, it doesn't even taste that good anymore.

Exercise is another area that can easily become a guilt trap for me. I know I should do some form of physical exercise every day, but I also know my schedule and myself well enough that I can't adhere to a strict daily commitment. Instead, my goal is to exercise three days per week. Some weeks I exercise more than three days, and other weeks it's a real effort, but I don't carry a load of guilt when I don't get it done.

Responding to Guilt

Should we feel guilty for overeating? Is overeating sin? Should we feel guilty if we are overweight? We could fill the rest of this book debating those questions and come up with some great Scripture references that would appear to support both sides. But, instead let's establish some principles on which I trust we can all agree.

- God created and designed our bodies, and we are responsible to care for them properly.
- The majority of our weight problems are the result of eating more food than our bodies need and/or eating foods that are not healthy.
- God has designed and provided the foods we need for the proper nutrition of our bodies.

- Most of us do not get as much physical exercise as we should.
- When we exercise and give our bodies proper nutrition, we are more physically and mentally productive for the Lord.

Our response to guilt is important. The healthy response is to *acknowledge* any wrong behavior or thinking pattern, *confess* it to God, *ask* for and *accept* his forgiveness, and take positive steps to *change* our behavior. With forgiveness "…there is now no condemnation for those who are in Christ Jesus" (Romans 8:1).

A healthy response to guilt will motivate us to make an honest Biblical evaluation of our eating patterns and the condition of our physical bodies. If we respond correctly, that evaluation will produce a change in our thinking and behavior.

An unhealthy response to guilt can cause a person to wallow in self-condemnation and ultimately fall into depression. It may result in a cycle of wrong behavior, guilt, confession, and back to wrong behavior. Satan would like us to slip into this pattern, for that kind of thinking and behavior will eventually immobilize even the strongest Christian.

Fighting your battle of the bulge will require a lifelong commitment on your part. You may always struggle with food and portion temptations and your weight will sometimes fluctuate. But don't carry the burden of guilt and self-condemnation. Christ died to set you free. Accept his forgiveness and live a life of victory in him!

Changing Your Focus

The Bible says only God can judge the heart, and I would not dare to judge yours. I can only express how I personally changed myself. My goals and motives were not necessarily wrong in and of themselves. What made them wrong is that *people, events,* and even *I* had become foremost in my mind and life. I cared more about what I looked like to others than what my heart looked like to Christ. I cared more about what others thought of me than what Christ thought of me. I cared more about pleasing others than pleasing him.

I wish I could tell you my goals and motives became instantly pure and godly and have remained that way ever since. No, at times they are skewed. I put too much emphasis on my outward appearance and still try to impress others. I find myself thoroughly focused on my weight, and I set goals based on social events. I slip back into the old thinking and behavior patterns. But, now there is a difference. It doesn't take me as long to refocus my goals and motives on Christ and his purposes for me as it did before.

I've quit *focusing* on pleasing people, even the dearest people in my life. I cannot please everybody, but I can strive to please my Lord. His opinion is what matters.

I've quit *focusing* on events, for they will come and go, and after they're over, I find no one really cared how thin I was anyway. My relationships and opportunities for ministering to people at the events are far more important than trying to impress them by shedding a few pounds.

I've quit *focusing* on feeling good about myself. I want to feel good about taking care of the gifts God has given to me, including my body.

I've quit *focusing* on the long-range picture. I still have long-range goals, but I now take one week at a time, one day at a time, and one meal at a time. I can't hold onto tomorrow, for I only have today. I can't be obedient for the future, but I can be obedient for this moment.

The changes in my life didn't happen overnight; I'm still learning daily obedience. But through the process, God has blessed my life abundantly. My health and energy level has improved, my husband is thrilled with the weight I've lost, my children are enormously proud of me, my wardrobe has expanded because my clothes fit better, and friends have noticed and asked to be a part of the battle Bible study groups. At a recent reunion, several people asked what I was doing to lose weight, and as I shared what God was doing in my life, opportunities for ministry began to open. As a natural result of my obedience, God is meeting more goals than I had set for myself.

God Changes Motives

I know people who won't do the right thing until they have the proper attitude, motives, and goals because they feel they would be hypocritical. That's not a reason; it's an *excuse*. I know; I've used it myself. No matter what our motives, no matter what our goals, and no matter how we *feel* we still need to do what is right. "Anyone, then, who knows the good he ought to do and doesn't do it, sins" (James 4:17). If you only do what's right when you *feel* good about it, you will rarely accomplish anything.

One day my friend Pam and I were talking about our motives in regard to speaking opportunities. Pam, a missionary, is an excellent speaker. One minute she has the audience rolling in laughter, and the next moment they are reduced to tears. Whether she speaks for five minutes or forty-five minutes, her message is always interesting and inspiring. But Pam struggles with her motives. She wants them to be pure, and because she is often complimented on her speaking ability, pride sometimes creeps into her. She can be sidetracked if she thinks about the impression she's making on others rather than the message God wants to speak through her.

Should Pam quit speaking because her motives aren't always perfect? No. If she did that, she might never speak again!

Pam shared her concerns with another speaker and received excellent advice. "Keep speaking the message God has for you; tell him when you're not sure if your motives are right, and let him change them for you."

Let God take care of changing your motives. You take care of your obedience.

God Rewards Obedience

When people join our weekly battle groups, their initial motivation is simply to lose weight; it is the reward for which they are looking. But, as the weeks pass, they begin to understand that the battle *is not just about the weight*; healthy eating and exercise are only part of the war. It's a joy to watch as God transforms their motives and rewards their commitment with not only pounds lost, but with joy, peace, and contentment.

It takes character to be obedient, and obedience builds character. My goal now is to be obedient, and my motive is to please God. I want my legacy to be like that of Enoch in Hebrews 11:5: "...he had this testimony, that he pleased God." Will I *always* please God? No. Will my motives *always* be pure? No. But, those are goals for which I'm striving. Will you join me?

Prayer: Dear Lord, forgive me for putting other people, circumstances, and myself before you. I want my motives and goals to be your motives and goals for my entire life and especially in my daily eating. As I strive to be obedient to you each day, I look to you to transform my motives and goals. In Jesus' name, I pray. Amen.

Memory Verse: *"Brethren, I do not count myself to have apprehended; but one thing I do, forgetting those things which are behind and reaching forward to those things which are ahead. I press toward the goal for the prize of the upward call of God in Christ Jesus."* *Philippians 3:13-14*

Food for Thought

1. List some of your past motives for losing weight.
2. Are you harboring any false guilt?
3. Have you made any wrong vows or commitments from which you need to ask

God to release you?

4. How can you make positive changes in your motives and goals?

5. What rewards are you seeking for your obedience?

CHAPTER EIGHT

Knowing Your Commander in Chief

"Yet I am not ashamed, because I know whom I have
believed, and am convinced that he is able to guard
what I have entrusted to him for that day."
2 Timothy 1:12b

Chapter Eight

Knowing Your Commander in Chief

Not long ago I attended the Christian Booksellers Association trade show in Denver, and over lunch, I visited with an editor friend about my book. My friend, also named Mary, was intrigued with the battle concept, and we shared our mutual frustration over the amount of time we have spent thinking about dieting and food. We both agreed it's *definitely* a battle.

"Mary," I asked, "if you were to add up all the time you've wasted consumed with thinking about your weight, dieting, and what you're going to eat for your next meal, how many days or weeks would it total?"

Without hesitation, she responded, "Oh, no! Not days or weeks—years!"

Sadly, I had to admit that I, too, spent far too much of my life consumed with thoughts of food and dieting.

"You know, Mary," I said, "I can't help but believe I would know Christ more intimately if I had devoted even a small portion of that time to my relationship with him."

Mary and I are not the only ones who struggle with this problem. In our hectic American culture, we sometimes consume three hearty meals each day in addition to a snack—or two—or three. We skip meals because we're in a rush, or we want to "save up" for the next spread or dessert in which we plan to indulge. That overindulgence usually accompanies a promise to get back on track *tomorrow*. In the midst of this gluttony, we're already thinking about the next morsel that will give us a temporary feeling of satisfaction. Our lives seem to center around planning for food, buying food, fixing food, the anticipation of eating food, eating too much food, feeling guilty, confessing our overindulgence, and planning for our next diet. We live in a constant state of frustration, because our lives revolve around functions at home, at work, and at social gatherings where food is served.

I have a Jewish friend who has this problem under total control. He never overindulges, yet his ministry, in fact, nearly his whole life, consists of social events where food is served. He is often the guest at dinner parties given in his honor, and he frequently spends several days at a time with friends as an overnight guest where he is lavished with food. He can be seen ministering in wheat fields or vineyards, and it's not uncommon for him to assist fishermen on their vessels and then share a meal on the beach. He's even been known to host huge luncheons with guests numbering in the thousands. As a devout Jew, he faithfully observes the religious holidays and feasts with his family and close friends. He doesn't say *no* to invitations, but he does say *no* to overindulgence. He is the perfect model of how I should conduct myself at meal times.

Who is he? His name is Jesus Christ. Although he performed numerous miracles, many that involved food, and he could have instantaneously created all the delicacies he desired, he chose to be obedient to the heavenly Father and refrain from overindulgence. *That same choice is yours to make.*

But, Jesus is perfect, you say; I could never be like him. True, this side of heaven you will not be sinless, and you will not always be victorious in your battles. But through the Scriptures you can get a glimpse into his thinking and follow his example. With the power of the Holy Spirit, you can have victory over the sin and habits that bind you (Romans 7:24-25).

He Understands Your Pain

Perhaps you are experiencing a degree of emotional, spiritual, and even physical pain in your weight battle. You may want to wave the white flag of surrender, but stop! *Jesus understands.* His heart aches with you and for you when you are teased or ridiculed, shamed or humiliated. Through the very hurt from which you long to be free, he wants to draw you to himself. *Jesus understands.* In your suffering, he wants you to place your life alongside his. "Therefore let those who suffer according to the will of God commit their souls to him in doing well, as to a faithful Creator" (1 Peter 4:19). In your pain, turn *to* him, not *from* him. *Jesus understands.*

The Bible says Christ sympathizes with your weaknesses because he was tempted in every area just like you, yet he did not sin (Hebrews 4:15). He *knows* how you feel; he *knows* the temptations you face. "And God is faithful; he will not let you be tempted beyond what you can bear. But when you are tempted, he will also provide a way out so that you can stand up under it" (1 Corinthians 10:13). He was tempted and tested spiritually, physically, and emotionally every day of his life on earth, and yet *he chose obedience.*

As a child in Minnesota, I spent a great deal of time playing outside during the summer months. Minnesota is infamous for its man-eating mosquitoes, and my arms and legs frequently showed signs of their voracious appetites. I remember scratching those bites till I bled, and then, just as the sores began to scab over, I scratched till I bled again. I think Satan similarly picks at our pain. Just when we think we are beginning to heal from our battle wounds, he rips off the scab, and the pain begins again.

Are you a wounded, bloodied dieter? Have you tried every diet on the market, and you're tired of failing? Do you feel like you don't have the energy to try even once more?

That is *exactly* where the Lord wants you! Come to the cross—let Jesus anoint your wounds with the healing power of his love and forgiveness. Let him show you a path that leads to freedom and deliverance. Don't let Satan tear at your wounds any longer.

In the Trenches with Our Commander

Imagine you are lying in a trench in the midst of a battlefield; bullets and mortar are whizzing above your head. Suddenly, you realize you're all alone; all your comrades have deserted you, and the enemy is launching an all-out assault. You cry out, "Oh, God, help me!" And, that's exactly what he does. He snatches you from the clutches of the enemy and lifts you out of the trench. He sets you on higher ground to give you the advantage and together you go on to victory.

Not only does your commander in chief understand your pain and the trials and temptations you face, he longs to fight along side you. He wants to deliver you from the enemy. He isn't sitting in some heavenly war room passing down orders through his angels until they reach you on the battlefield; he communicates directly with you. He gives guidance through his Word and prayer, he gives power and strength through the Holy Spirit, and he arms you with weapons to fight your battles. He *is* and *gives* all you need for victory.

God will not just *do* for you on the battlefield; he will *be* for you on the battlefield. The Bible says he is:

Your Defense—"For You have been my defense and refuge in the day of my trouble" (Psalm 59:16).

Your Guide—"For this is God, our God forever and ever; He will be our guide even to death" (Psalm 48:14).

Your Foundation—"For no other foundation can anyone lay than that which is laid which is Jesus Christ" (1 Corinthians 3:11).

Your Rock, Fortress, Deliverer, Strength, Stronghold, Shield, Refuge, and Savior—"…The LORD is my rock and my fortress and my deliverer; the God of my strength, in whom I will trust; My shield and the horn of my salvation, My stronghold and my refuge; My Savior, You save me from violence" (2 Samuel 22:2-4).

Your Guard—"But the Lord is faithful, who will establish you and guard you from the evil one" (2 Thessalonians 3:3).

Your Shelter and Tower—"For You have been a shelter for me, A strong tower from the enemy" (Psalm 61:3).

Why would you want to serve under any other commander? Why would you want to give one inch to the enemy?

> *You are not without defense—he will guard you.*
> *You are not without direction—he will guide you.*
> *You are not without stability—he is your foundation.*
> *You are not without weapons—he is your shield and sword.*
> *You are not left on an open battlefield—he is your fortress and shelter.*

Removing Barriers

Balancing marriage, family, and ministry is sometimes a difficult task for my husband and me. In order to function happily and productively, we need to work at keeping open lines of communication. However, sometimes we do and say things to each other that are hurtful or offensive, and a wall of anger and resentfulness rises between us. Usually, we settle our differences quickly, but we can both be stubborn and foolishly hang on to things that create a rift in our relationship. To restore oneness, the person who is wrong (sometimes it's both of us) needs to acknowledge the fault and ask forgiveness. Because we're human and have many faults, making amends is an ongoing process. As our relationship has grown, we offend less often, and we are able to break down the barriers more quickly, restoring fellowship. Likewise, you and I must have a good relationship and open communication with our commander in chief.

The Bible calls our offenses against God *sin*. Sin puts a barrier or wedge between God and us, hindering our relationship with him, just as unresolved conflict does in our personal relationships. We can break down the barrier and restore a right relationship with God: "If we confess our sins, He is faithful and just and will forgive us our sins and purify us from all unrighteousness" (1 John 1:9).

Do you have issues with God you need to confess? Don't stubbornly hang on to them; acknowledge your sins and remove the barrier. Do you have unresolved conflicts with other people? That, too, can build a wall between you and God. Sin that has not been dealt with will be a hindrance in your battle of the bulge, like a burden holding you back. You need to make a habit of cleaning the slate throughout each day. Psalm 66:18 says if we don't confess our sins, God will not hear our prayers. You cannot battle as *one* with a barrier between you and God, or you and another person. Are you holding back in any way? Are you bitter at yourself, another person, or God over past failures? Have you refused to accept the body God gave you? Do you harbor resentment toward someone?

We all have problems with sin in our lives (Romans 3:23), but don't let it hold you back from victory. Satan may be accusing you daily before the throne of God, but Jesus Christ is your advocate who defends and forgives you (1 John 2:1). Examine yourself, talk with God, and remove the barriers.

Trust and Obey

When my children were growing up there were times when they asked *why*, and the only answer I was at liberty to give at that moment was, *because I said so*. Before I had children of my own, I promised myself I would never use that phrase; instead, I would patiently offer a reasonable explanation to their questions. But, as a parent, I found there were times when my children needed to obey without explanation. They needed to trust me; they needed to have faith in my judgment. It had to be enough for them to know I loved them and had their best interest at heart.

There will be times in your life when you will have to trust God's judgment by faith and obey him without understanding why he is asking for your obedience. He is God, and he is under no obligation to explain his reasons. It must be enough to know the *who* without knowing the *why*. It must be enough to know he loves you and has your best interest at heart. "…The judgments of the LORD are true and righteous altogether. More to be desired are they than gold, yea than much fine gold; sweeter also than honey and the honeycomb. Moreover by them Your servant is warned, And in keeping them there is great reward" (Psalm 19:9-11).

In boot camp, new recruits learn to obey their drill sergeant without delay and without question for there will be no time for discussion and explanation on the battlefield. Questions raise fear and doubt, and waste valuable time. Hesitation to obey can and will result in casualties. A good soldier tries to see the battle the way his commanding officer sees it, but when the way is not clear, the soldier's confidence and trust in his superior must be sufficient to merit obedience.

Likewise, we must not hesitate to act in obedience to what we know to be right and true. We don't have a drill sergeant, but we do have God in the person of the Holy Spirit to teach and guide us. As we choose to be obedient in our choices of healthy foods and reasonable portions, doubts, fears, and failure will give way to confidence and victory.

Throughout the Biblical history of Israel, God gave a straightforward pattern his people were to follow in battle and every other area of life:

1. Seek him
2. Obey his plan
3. Reap the victory
4. Worship him

This, too, is God's plan for you. *There is no room for partial obedience.* I once heard a speaker say something I've never forgotten; *incomplete obedience is disobedience.* God knows what is best for you and wants you to follow his plan for your lives. He has presented his guidelines in the Bible, and he expects you to *trust* and *obey.* When you follow his instructions, you will be victorious. But when you deviate from his plan in any way, you will experience defeat and judgment.

God's Battle Plans

Sometimes God's battle plans followed standard military procedure, but often as not, they were unique and unorthodox.

Who would have thought the way to defeat the powerful Egyptian army was by obediently crossing the Red Sea between two great walls of water?

Who would have thought the mighty walls of Jericho would collapse after the warriors and priests of Israel obediently marched around the city once a day for six days and then seven times on the seventh day with the priests blowing their trumpets and a final shout from the people?

Who would have thought by killing a fearsome nine-foot nine-inch giant, an obedient young shepherd boy would initiate the needed courage for a frightened king and a timid army to defeat the powerful Philistines?

Who would have thought twelve simple men would change the course of history through obediently proclaiming the message of an obscure prophet who defeated his enemy by his death on a cross and his resurrection three days later?

Incredible stories? *Amazing stories!*

We are quick to believe that God will work miraculously and victoriously in the lives of others, but we doubt that he will do the same for us, especially in something as insignificant as appetite control. Yet that is precisely his desire. He wants to work *in* us, *through* us, and *with* us as we obediently face our daily battles with food, appetite, emotions, and more. Insignificant? Not at all! What could be more significant than a healthy body charged with physical, emotional, and spiritual energy ready to serve Christ?

Learning to Think Like Christ

Melody was in one of my first battle groups, and though she faithfully attended each Monday afternoon for months, she only lost a few pounds. Her focus was still primarily on the weight, and she did not quite grasp the relationship between obedience to God and her eating habits.

One day Melody came to class and, before I had a chance to open my Bible, she asked us to turn to 1 Peter 4:1-3. She read, "Therefore, since Christ suffered for us in the flesh, arm yourselves also with the same mind, for he who has suffered in the flesh has ceased from sin, that he no longer should live the rest of his time in the flesh for the lusts of men, but for the will of God. For we have spent *enough* of our past lifetime in doing the will of the Gentiles—when we walked in lewdness, lusts, drunkenness, revelries, drinking parties, and abominable idolatries" (emphasis mine).

"Girls," Melody said, "do you see that word *enough*? Well, *I've had enough*! I've spent *enough* of my past life overeating and living in disobedience—no more!"

Melody was growing closer to Christ as she began to think more like him, and she went on to lose nearly forty pounds! But, she didn't come to that place overnight, and it was not an easy journey. It took time, effort, seeking, and study for Melody to think like Christ. Melody would be the first to say there are days when she still struggles, but she knows the battle *is not just about the weight.*

Are you to the point you've had *enough* pain and frustration reaped from disobedience? Are you ready to change your thinking and thus your behavior? It's true God is gracious and merciful and forgiving, and you can always start again tomorrow. But, remember, *you only have this moment to be obedient to this battle.*

Each time you don't surrender to the will of your heavenly Father, you are giving up ground to the enemy. You are believing the same lie that Satan used with Eve in the Garden of Eden: *you are in control, you are like God* (Genesis 3:5). God has redeemed you from the hand of the enemy (Psalm 107:1, 2); don't live any longer in the old way. Tell the enemy you have had *enough*!

The Fear of Obedience

The summer I was five years old, my family packed into our red Rambler station wagon and headed west. For the next few weeks, we visited tourist attractions like the Grand Canyon, the Great Salt Lake, Yellowstone and Glacier National Parks, Deadwood, Wall Drug, Boot Hill, and more. But, to me, the highlight of that trip came each evening when we checked into our motel. As soon as we ate supper, all four of us kids headed off to the swimming pool.

I didn't know how to swim, but I loved to splash and play and jump in the shallow end of the pool. When my father joined us, he'd hold out his arms just below the surface of the water. I'd lie across his arms kicking and swinging my arms, pretending I could swim. Sometimes he stood in the deep end of the pool with his arms outstretched and called, "Jump, Mary! I'll catch you." I was fearful because the water was deep, but trust in my father overcame my fear. I plunged into the water, confident I was safe in his arms.

Your heavenly Father is holding out his arms to you, and he wants your trust in him to overcome your fears; he wants you to rest in his arms. Why not take the plunge?

Obedience to a Person, Not a Program

Most people in our battle groups have successfully lost weight—some have lost a few pounds, others have lost fifty, seventy-five, or more. As friends and family notice their weight loss, they inevitably ask, "What diet are you using?" Of course, the answer is the majority do not use a specific diet. Rather, they follow a personal eating plan that includes developing self-control and godly character qualities, eating healthier food in smaller portions, and exercising. Their eating plan is based on individual tastes, lifestyle, and budget. As their relationship with Christ matures, they learn to apply Biblical principles to their battle. They learn obedience and commitment to a *person*, the Lord Jesus Christ, not a *program*.

I spent years trying to commit to and follow the guidelines set forth in diet programs, but I continued to fail. I am now committed to a *person*, not a diet. I'm in a *relationship*, not on a regiment. I obey with *gratefulness*, not obligation. I'm no longer a *prisoner*, I'm set free.

Obedience is a choice—*your* choice.

Just before Joshua died, he spoke to the children of Israel and encouraged them to stop wavering in their loyalties. He left them with the challenge of a choice. "Now therefore, fear the LORD, serve Him in sincerity and in truth, and put away the gods which your fathers served on the other side of the River and in Egypt. Serve the LORD! And if it seems evil to you to serve the LORD, *choose for yourselves this day whom you will serve*…But as for me and my house, we will serve the LORD" (Joshua 24:14-15, emphasis mine).

Our three children are now grown and on their own, but they still occasionally phone home and seek our advice. I'll admit it makes me feel good that they care what we think; after all, we raised them. Did you ever stop to think how your heavenly Father feels when you stop to ask his advice about your life? After all, he made you.

Life is not about *your* plan for *your* life to fulfill *your* desires. Fulfilling *your* selfish desires is why you have a weight problem. Take the time to create and prepare a healthy eating and exercise plan. Seek God, ask him, and obey him. He is worthy of your obedience and praise, and *his* plan for your life will give you victory.

Prayer: Dear Lord, thank you for *providing* all I need for battle and *being* all I need for battle. Forgive me for allowing people, circumstances, personal pleasure, and even my appetite to come between you and me. I now want to offer you now the sacrifice of my obedience. I commit to face my battles with you one day at a time, one meal at a time, and one moment at a time. Thank you for your gift of the Holy Spirit to remind me when I fail. Thank you for your gift of the Bible to guide me on your path for my life. In Jesus' name, I pray. Amen.

Memory Verse: *"Yet I am not ashamed, because I know whom I have believed, and am convinced that he is able to guard what I have entrusted to him for that day."* 2 Timothy 1:12b

Food for Thought

We can be stubborn and insist on doing things our own way, but eventually we find that God's way leads to joy, peace, and victory.

Read Joshua 5:13-6:2 and note four important principles.

"Now when Joshua was near Jericho, he looked up and saw a man standing in front of him with a drawn sword in his hand. Joshua went up to him and asked, 'Are you for us or for our enemies?'

"'Neither,' he replied, 'but as commander of the army of the LORD I have now come.' Then Joshua fell facedown to the ground in reverence, and asked him, 'What message does my Lord have for his servant?'

"The Commander of the LORD's army replied, 'Take off your sandals, for the place where you are standing is holy.' And Joshua did so.

"Now Jericho was tightly shut up because of the Israelites. No one went out and no one came in.

"Then the LORD said to Joshua, 'See, I have delivered Jericho into your hands, along with its king and its fighting men.'"

1. You are not alone. Joshua 5:13 and 14
2. You are second in command. Joshua 5:14
3. Consecration precedes conquest. Joshua 5:15
4. The power of God is greater than the problem of man. Joshua 6:1 and 2

USING YOUR WEAPONS

"For though we live in the world, we do not wage war as the world does. The weapons we fight with are not the weapons of the world. On the contrary, they have divine power to demolish strongholds. We demolish arguments and every pretension that sets itself up against the knowledge of God, and we take captive every thought to make it obedient to Christ."
2 Corinthians 10:3-5

CHAPTER NINE

Using Your Weapons

The winter of 1777-1778 at Valley Forge, Pennsylvania, was nearly the end for George Washington's Continental army. For more than two years the soldiers had suffered one defeat after another, and now the troops were cold, sick, hungry, and dejected. As Christmas approached, so did the discharge date for thousands of men. What was Washington to do? How could he possibly hold this disheartened, ragtag army together? Incredibly, following an impassioned plea from their commander in chief, a majority of the men chose to remain.

On February 23, 1778, additional relief came to Washington by way of a former Prussian army officer named Baron Friedrich Wilhelm Augustus von Steuben. Von Steuben was appalled by what he saw at Valley Forge—squalor, sickness, discouragement, lack of discipline, and ineffectual use of weaponry. His work was cut out for him, but his experience in the Prussian army had prepared him well.

Victory in battle in the eighteenth century largely depended on which side could get off the first round of shots, reload the quickest, and get off another round. Battles were fought at close range and skilled, rapid use of weaponry was of primary importance. The Continental army was largely composed of farmers and merchants who knew how to hunt for food and protect their homes and families from Indian attacks, but they were unskilled in military warfare.

Baron von Steuben introduced training techniques that not only changed the course of the war, but also were used in the U.S. military for years to come. He drilled the soldiers until the act of loading, firing, and reloading was automatic. He organized a training program that taught men to lead and train other men in warfare technique, especially on how to effectively use their weapons. The assemblage of farmers and merchants became an army under von Steuben's guidance.

What made the difference? The soldiers were the same ragged, barefoot recruits, and the weapons were the same clumsy, single shot muskets. So, why did the Continental army finally begin to experience victory? Preparation, planning, and training! They developed structure and discipline, and they learned how to effectively use the weapons and ammunition they already possessed. *Von Steuben taught them techniques that were superior to those of the enemy.*

Have you entered the battlefield of weight loss unprepared? Do you know what weapons are available to you, or are you making clumsy attempts with a single-shot musket, only to find yourself wounded and defeated before you can reload and get off the next round? Do you feel bombarded by a tank while you watch your own shots bounce off the enemy like tiny pellets from a BB gun?

Perhaps like me, you entered your battle of the bulge armed with fad diet plans, good intentions, and even the Bible and a prayer. In the following pages, you will discover that you have a host of weapons and ammunition in your arsenal, but you have not adequately trained and learned to use them effectively. You will discover that daily drilling with your weapons will make them familiar and easy to use. *You will find that your weapons are superior to those of the enemy.*

A New Kind of Warfare

Until recently, our military strategists were accustomed to a fair amount of certainty when it came to warfare tactics. They knew precisely who the enemy was and his country of origin. They could gauge his approximate time of attack, what his weapons would be, and they knew what his uniform looked like. The 9/11 attacks on the Twin Towers and the Pentagon and the tragic airliner crash in Pennsylvania changed all that.

We are now fighting a different kind of enemy and a different kind of war— terrorism. These enemy "soldiers" live next door and are dressed like you and me, or they hide in desert caves clothed in flowing robes. They are from Iraq, Afghanistan, the Philippines, Pakistan, Europe, and, alarmingly, even the United States. They use our own airliners as weapons against us, and they have no regard for human life, not even their own. They have caused division among our citizens and political parties, and among our country and other nations. Terrorists bring panic and disorder, and if they can create fear and confusion, they are well on their way to victory.

Like a human terrorist, Satan breeds confusion and doubt and causes division. He is everywhere, and he is nowhere. He has no regard for the God of the universe or God's children, and he tries to use our own weapons against us. He is sly, subversive, and clever. He knows our weak points and is familiar with our weapons. Satan is a formidable enemy, and though he may think he is well on his way to defeating us, we have an even more formidable God who gives us victory in battle through the Lord Jesus Christ!

The Bible—Our Field Manual

One reason the war against terrorism is so frightening is that there is no defined frontline to defend. We don't know from where or when an attack will come; therefore, we must depend on first-rate intelligence. In our battle of the bulge we too must depend on first-rate intelligence, and the Bible is our source, for it is within its pages we learn about our enemy—his warfare tactics and how he can be defeated. It is our field manual for battle.

The Bible tells us God's purpose for our lives, and it is where we get knowledge, wisdom, and understanding. It is not only a book of history, prophecy, science, poetry, and practical lessons on life, it contains God's message to the world. It is a living book, and the means by which God chose to communicate his thoughts, desires, and plans for his children. It is a powerful book that has influenced human history unlike any other. "For the word of God is *living and powerful*, and sharper than any two-edged sword, piercing even to the division of soul and spirit, and of joints and marrow, and is a discerner of the thoughts and intents of the heart" (Hebrews 4:12, emphasis mine).

The Bible is *not* a book about weight loss, yet within its pages we find the battle principles needed to guide us to victory. God's "...divine power has given us everything we need for life and godliness through our knowledge of him...so that through them you may participate in the divine nature and escape the corruption in the world caused by evil desires" (2 Peter 1:3-4). Where do we find the knowledge of him? Where do we find the way to be partakers of his divine nature? The answer is: in the Bible. That is why we must daily search God's Word for direction and turn to him in prayer for strength.

Armed and Ready—He Provides, I Obey

When a soldier is wearing his uniform and holding his weapon, it's an indication that he's ready for battle. But he must do more than just *look* the part. A battle-ready soldier is one who has prepared not only his body, but his mind and emotions as well. He has the physical endurance to withstand an attack or to launch an assault. He has the mental and emotional stamina to promptly obey orders without question, and he will fight regardless of fear. He not only knows his enemy's tactics, he knows which weapons are suitable to defend or attack.

We too need to be battle ready, for our battle of the bulge is more than just a physical, mental, and emotional conflict; it has a very real spiritual element. Satan is an elusive enemy who wants to keep our focus on our physical appearance, what we will eat for our next meal, and what others think about us. He will use any means within his power to keep our focus off the Lord.

A spiritual enemy like Satan cannot be defeated with bullets and tanks, so God provides battle plans, armor, and weapons to ensure victory. Ephesians 6:10-17 is the consummate Bible reference on spiritual warfare. These verses not only describe the wicked cunning of the enemy, but also the means by which he may be defeated.

"Finally, be strong in the Lord and in his mighty power. Put on the full armor of God so that you can take your stand against the devil's schemes. For our struggle is not against flesh and blood, but against the rulers, against the authorities, against the powers of this dark world and against the spiritual forces of evil in the heavenly realms. Therefore put on the full armor of God, so that when the day of evil comes, you may be able to stand your ground, and after you have done everything, to stand. Stand firm then, with the belt of truth buckled around your waist, with the breastplate of righteousness in place, and with your feet fitted with the readiness that comes from the gospel of peace. In addition to all this, take up the shield of faith, with which you can extinguish all the flaming arrows of the evil one. Take the helmet of salvation and the sword of the Spirit, which is the word of God."

Left to ourselves, we are weak, but God does not leave us to stand and battle alone. In verse ten, he reminds us our strength and power are in *him*. The passage tells us *his* armor will give the strength we need to stand against and oppose, or resist the enemy. God is the provider of *all* we need to win our battles. But, note that although God *provides* all that we need for victory, *he does not dress us*. Seven times he refers to receiving or putting on the armor, but he does not do it for us. *We are responsible to take the armor and put it on, then activate our weapons through obedience.*

As a Christian for many years, I had often used God's weapons, but I had never applied them to my weight. I might have *looked* battle ready—after all, I was a pastor's wife, taught Bible studies, and helped prepare others for life's battles—but when it came to my weight war, it was as if I was only wearing the uniform and holding a rifle loaded with blanks. I wanted God to dress me and hand me the weapons, and I wanted him to fight the battle for me. That's not how God's army functions. He provides his strength and his power, and the weapons and the armor, but *I* have to get dressed and go into battle. *I* have to be obedient each day, each moment, each meal.

Satan would have us believe that he is too powerful an enemy for us to combat, and that the weapons God provides are not adequate. But, "...the weapons we fight with are not the weapons of the world. On the contrary, they have divine power to demolish strongholds" (2 Corinthians 10:4). God doesn't promise to deliver us *from* the battle, but he does promise to deliver us *in* the battle. He has protection for us and weapons to defeat Satan no matter how or when the enemy attacks for "...in all these things we are more than conquerors through him who loved us" (Romans 8:37). Unlike the Continental army, which was always short of rifles, ammunition, cannon, and gunpowder, you and I are never short of weapons unless *we* neglect to pick them up and use them.

When I was a young Christian reading about the armor and weapons in Ephesians, I felt intimidated and inadequate, questioning whether I would make a good soldier. I knew about the weapons, but I didn't fully comprehend their true power. I was confident about the *helmet of salvation,* for I had accepted Christ as my Savior when I was twelve years old. As a teenager I learned to clearly share my faith with others, so I knew my feet were shod with the *readiness of the gospel.* But what about the *belt of truth,* the *breastplate of righteousness,* the *shield of faith,* and the *sword of the Spirit;* how was I to put on the armor and use the weapons?

I decided to list the armor and weapons and see what the Scriptures had to say about each one. I found:

- In John 14: 6 that *Jesus* is the *truth.*
- In 2 Corinthians 5:21 that our *righteousness* is in *Christ.*
- In 1 Corinthians 15:1-4 that the death, burial, and resurrection of *Jesus Christ* is described as the *gospel.*
- In Hebrews 12:2 that the author and finisher of our *faith* is *Jesus Christ.*
- In Luke 2:30 that *Jesus* is our *salvation.*
- In John 1:1, 2 and 14 that *Jesus Christ* is the *Word* in the flesh.

Jesus Christ doesn't just *provide* our armor, our weapons, our strength, and our power; he *is* our armor, our weapons, and our strength and power. 1 Corinthians 9:7 asks the question, "Who serves as a soldier at his own expense?" The answer is *no one.* He is and gives all I need. I am not adequate—but he is. I will never be spiritual enough—but he is. When I am obedient to one command, he gives me strength to follow the next. Each small step of obedience gives me more strength and power. I don't have to worry about my worthiness, spirituality, or godliness; I just have to be obedient one step at a time. I just have to do the next right thing, and God will take care of equipping me for the battle.

"…Let us put aside the deeds of darkness and put on the armor of light. Let us behave decently…*clothe yourselves with the Lord Jesus Christ,* and do not think about how to gratify the desires of the sinful nature" (Romans 13:12-14, emphasis mine). When I *put on* Jesus Christ through obedience to his Word, I cannot fail!

Prayer: Developing Open Lines of Communication

"And pray in the Spirit on all occasions with all kinds of prayers and requests. With this

in mind, be alert and always keep on praying for all the saints." Ephesians 6:18

On March 19, 1972, Lieutenant Hiroo Onoda emerged from the Philippine jungle on the island of Lubang, nearly thirty years after he was deployed by the Japanese army to conduct guerrilla warfare during World War II. Due to severed lines of communication, he was never officially told the war had ended. For twenty-nine years, he ate coconuts and bananas while evading search parties he thought were enemy scouts. Lieutenant Onoda and his commanding officers had poor lines of communication.

I'm so glad that our prayer line of communication is never broken or jammed, for prayer is our two-way radio with God, how we partner with him in warfare and in fellowship. It is so vital to life's battles that Jesus made it a priority in his earthly life and ministry. He knew the power of prayer and even instructed his disciples to ask for deliverance from Satan (Matthew 6:13). Because prayer is our most devastating and powerful weapon in defeating the enemy, our lines of communication with our commander in chief, the Lord Jesus Christ, must remain open and secure at all times (1 Thessalonians 5:17).

Prayer Is Not a Magic Wand

In difficult situations, I have sometimes tried to use prayer as a magic wand or a tool to manipulate God into giving me my own way. But prayer is not a means by which to make spiritual bargains, nor is it a divine shopping cart to fill with selfish requests. Rather, it is how we communicate with him at any time and in any situation. Prayer is how we praise and glorify God, and it is the means by which we cry out to him in trouble and pain. It is how we make petitions for others and how we present personal prayer requests.

Sincere, godly praying requires not only *talking* to God, but also *listening* to him—it is a *two-way* conversation. And, listening to God, nearly always requires us to make changes in our behavior—sometimes painful and difficult changes. But, that's what obedience involves—prayer, listening, and change. God speaks primarily to us through the Bible under the guidance of the Holy Spirit, but he also uses other people and circumstances to let us know his will for our lives. (People can be deceiving and circumstances can be misleading, so be careful that counsel from those sources is *always* aligned with Scripture.)

I knew in my heart that if I really listened to what God was saying, it would demand work and changes in my self-centered lifestyle. But I didn't want to make changes in my eating or exercise habits, so I tried to pray God into miraculously doing it for me. I presented him with my requests and then added *thy will be done* as a postscript as if I really wanted his will instead of mine. What I was actually trying to do is manipulate God into forcing me to stick with a diet.

My dieting prayers were one-way, ineffective cries of self-centered frustration. I prayed things like, "Lord, if you'll just make me sick for a few days so that I lose five or ten pounds, I promise I will keep the weight off." Naturally, I wanted this ill health to be temporary, and I expected God to bless me with excellent health the rest of the time.

Or, "Lord, I think you made my metabolism too slow. Could you speed it up?" Of course, I didn't want to take the initiative to eat less food and exercise regularly.

And, best of all, "Lord, could you please take away my appetite and my desire for chocolate and cheesecake?" I didn't want to develop self-control and discipline, and refrain from eating unhealthy foods.

I'm so glad God didn't answer those foolish prayers the way I wanted. If he had, I would have forfeited my health and the pleasure of enjoying the marvelous foods he's provided. Most of all, I would not have learned the value of developing godly character.

Finally, "in my distress I called to the LORD; I cried to my God for help. From his temple he heard my voice; my cry came before him, into his ears" (Psalm 18:6). I asked God to forgive me for neglecting my body and his gift of healthy food. I asked him to show me the godly character I needed to develop while I sought wisdom and understanding as to how to effectively use the armor and weapons he had provided.

Guarding Your Mind

We lived in Alamogordo, New Mexico, near Holloman Air Force Base for several years and frequently visited friends who were stationed there. A fence surrounded the base, and the gatehouse entrance was guarded twenty-four hours a day by a sentry who stopped each vehicle to verify the visitor's name, purpose of the visit, and vehicle license plate number. The guard was placed at the entrance to keep out any person who might be a threat to the personnel, the equipment, or any sensitive information on the base. He was in place for protection and security, and in the event of the need for backup or any other problems, the sentry had a radio or telephone with which he could call for help.

You, too, need to place a sentry at the entrance of your mind for protection against anything that might be a threat to your physical, mental, emotional, and spiritual well being, for the mind is where battles begin. You must set a fence, or boundary, around your mind to protect yourself from any influence that may be a threat. Prayer is the means by which you can call out to God for backup; it is like placing a guard at the gatehouse of your mind to provide protection from the enemy. "Do not be anxious about anything, but in everything, by prayer and petition, with thanksgiving, present your requests to God. And the peace of God which transcends all understanding, will *guard your hearts and your minds in Christ Jesus*" (Philippians 4:6-7, emphasis mine).

The word *guard* sets forth the idea of watching at a gate in advance for spies, and to hem in and protect. But, prayer is not a passive guard. Just as the sentry at the Air Force base was always alert for danger, you must be watchful, prepared, and ready to respond to anything that may endanger you. "Be self-controlled and alert. Your enemy the devil prowls around like a roaring lion looking for someone to devour" (1 Peter 5:8). An attack or temptation may come in the form of food, circumstances, or a person, but the way you respond to the attack will be determined in your mind. You can help guard your mind by avoiding people, places, and circumstances that affect you in a negative way or bring unnecessary temptation into your life.

During time of war, a country is termed *occupied* when a foreign power takes over control of the government. What do you allow to *occupy* or control your mind? What negative influences do you allow into your thoughts? Are you filling your mind with good things, godly things? "Finally, brethren, whatever things are true, whatever things are noble, whatever things are just, whatever things are pure, whatever things are lovely, whatever things are of good report, if there is any virtue and if there is anything praiseworthy—meditate on these things" (Philippians 4:8).

You guard your mind by controlling what you allow into it by way of your five senses—what you see, taste, smell, hear, and touch. That may sound simple, but in this day and age it takes a concerted effort to sift what you see and hear. Consider the movies, Internet, and television programs you view. Who are your close associates and friends? What books do you read? How often do you read your Bible and attend church? How do you spend your free time? All these things and more will affect how you approach your battle and how effectively you use your weapons. What you allow to pass through the entrance gate of your mind will come out by way of your words, actions, and attitude. What *occupies* your mind will *control* your mind. "For as he thinks in his heart, so is he" (Proverbs 23:7).

Mealtime Prayers

When I was a little girl, our family said a prayer before each meal, and that practice has carried on into my own family. But too often it's something we do just because we're supposed to do it. Mealtimes can be a difficult battleground, and they are too important to brush off with a speedy, repetitive prayer. Yet, that's what many mealtime prayers are. "Father, thank you for this food and bless it to our bodies. In Jesus' name, I pray. Amen." Let's eat!

Consider the power and strength you might garner from a prayer like this: "Heavenly Father, thank you for the employment and finances that provided this meal, and thank you for those who prepared the food. Please join us in fellowship and may our conversation honor you. We offer our bodies as a sacrifice to you as it says in Romans 12:1 and we pray our conduct will please you. Thank you for the portion of this food that you want us to eat, and we commit to consume only what we require to satisfy our needs. May we glorify you today in all that we eat and drink and in our bodily exercise. In Jesus' name, we pray. Amen."

I don't think you would have a difficult time with gluttony after a prayer like that, do you? And it only takes about thirty seconds.

Using the Weapons We Have at Hand

When the giant Goliath derided and challenged the army of Israel, King Saul's choice of weapon was a sword, but David chose a slingshot. David and Saul had the same enemy and the same God, but they had different plans and different weapons. Saul was skilled with a sword, shield, and mail, but sat in his tent immobilized by fear and didn't use his weapons. David too was skilled with his weapon, but he perused the situation, applied his weapon to the challenge, and won the victory.

You and I will be challenged by the same enemy (Satan), but he will not attack or contend with us in the same manner. Because we will each face somewhat different temptations, the enemy will seek to attack us where we are uniquely the most vulnerable. We each face different challenges—bodies with diverse physical needs regarding food and exercise, minds and emotions that respond in distinctive ways—and we are each at varied levels in our spiritual walk with Christ. But we do have the same God, and though we may each take a different approach to our battles and use different weapons, we all are guaranteed victory through obedience to Christ.

How do you know which weapons to use? First, consider from where and when you are being attacked. Learn to use weapons that are appropriate to each battle—those that will adequately subdue the enemy. A bazooka isn't necessary to kill a rabbit when a .22 rifle will do the job. On the other hand, don't use a BB gun when you need a tank. You will face attacks that can be surmounted simply by pausing and asking yourself if you really need or want the food. Other attacks will require bringing out the heavy artillery—

reading your Bible, praying, quoting Scripture, or calling your battle buddy. Attacks can come at any time, and you must always be prepared with the right weapons.

Our Arsenal of Weapons

In addition to our spiritual weapons, we have physical, mental, and emotional weapons at our disposal. Consider the list below as you plan your offense and defense. You may find ideas you never before considered, and you may want to add your own ideas to the list.

- The **bathroom scale** should not be viewed as a foe, but as an ally to buoy you as you lose each pound. Rejoice with your battle buddy and praise God for each pound lost. When you're up a pound or two, use your scale as a reminder to get back on course.

- **Water** cleanses your system, hydrates your body, quenches thirst, and helps squelch hunger. (Other liquids are *not* a substitute for water.) Most weight-loss programs suggest drinking forty-eight to sixty-four ounces of water each day.

- Trying to lose weight without **exercising** is like having a gun without bullets— you may be able to use the gun as a club, but it's much more effective when you can shoot it. Exercise helps strengthen your bones and immune system, tones muscles, burns calories, relieves stress, and increases your metabolism. Not only will you lose weight more quickly with exercise, you will have a healthier body.

- Be armed with a well-planned **shopping list** when you enter the grocery store. It's like a piece of armor to protect you from impulse buying. Do most of your food shopping from the perimeter of the store where you will find fresh fruits and vegetables, dairy products, whole grain breads, and lean meats. Fresh healthy foods are not only God's gift to us for our pleasure and mutual fellowship, but they also ward off illness.

- Having **healthy snacks** available will curb mindless eating and munching on unhealthy, fattening foods. Most afternoons I have a hunger surge around 3:00, so I have *planned* and *prepared* to drink a cup of hot tea and eat some raisins. When I feel like chewing on something, I bring out the carrots and celery sticks. When I have a craving for something salty, I take a few pretzels out of the bag and immediately put the rest away to avoid further temptation.

- Sift through your collection of **diet and health books**. A prescribed diet that is *healthy and balanced* in all the food groups may be the plan God wants you to follow. If you have doubts or questions, check with your doctor.
- Find a **doctor** and/or a registered dietitian who understands nutrition and has the time and patience to work with you. I believe your doctor is an influence and authority God has placed in your life; use his or her knowledge and ask questions.
- **Church friends and family** are important to keep you accountable. Enlist at least one friend (battle buddy) and be mutually accountable. The enemy would like nothing better than to isolate you, but remember, there is strength in numbers. "Though one may be overpowered, two can defend themselves. A cord of three strands is not quickly broken" (Ecclesiastes 4:12).
- The *Planning for the Battle of the Bulge* companion workbook/journal is a great resource to keep you organized and accountable. It includes a daily devotional guide for an entire year. You can plan for upcoming battles, record daily victories and defeats, and plan your meals. It is user-friendly and can be completed in just a few minutes each day.
- Commit **Scripture verses to memory and meditate** on them throughout the day. I don't mean the mediation of emptying your mind and allowing anything and everything into it, but rather the *filling* of your mind with God's Word. When you commit Scripture to memory, you can recall it at any time and for every battle. "Oh, how I love your law! I meditate on it all day long" (Psalm 119:97).
- **Christian music** is an effective weapon to lift your spirits especially if you are prone to emotional eating during times of stress or depression. "Speak to one another with psalms, hymns and spiritual songs. Sing and make music in your heart to the Lord" (Ephesians 5:19).
- Review your daily **victories and defeats**. Rejoice in victories, but don't allow yourself to become complacent in your victories. Encourage yourself by the character you've developed and the pounds you've lost. Don't wallow in defeats; rather learn to turn them into future victories.

Using Satan's Weapons Against Him

Chocolate cake, pie, cheesecake, and other delicacies may seem like Satan's deadliest weapons, but I believe he is as much, or more, destructive when he attacks your emotions with fears and doubts. Fear and doubt will quickly turn to discouragement, and discouragement will lead to failure. By preparing for these attacks and turning those negative weapons back against the enemy, you can help guard your mind.

Turn to the Lord in prayer when you feel discouraged. Find a way to serve another person or do something constructive when you are bored. Eat God's gift of fresh fruit when you're tempted with a dessert. Remind yourself of God's faithfulness when you doubt. Rest in the peace your Savior offers when you are frustrated.

Satan's offers—fad diets, pills, powders, wraps, and often dangerous and unnecessary surgeries—are tempting, but are only temporary solutions. Dependence on those weapons is like a soldier running onto a battlefield with only a toy gun for protection—it's a suicide mission!

The enemy wants you to compare yourself with movie stars, body builders, and even close friends and associates so you will be dissatisfied with your body, God's gift. He wants you to fail and become frustrated, angry, and discouraged. God wants you to compare yourself only to what you can be when you *clothe yourself*, or *put on* the Lord Jesus Christ. He wants you to succeed because he loves you and knows that the only way to complete joy, peace, and contentment is by receiving the gifts he offers.

Don't be discouraged if you are not immediately adept at using your weapons; it takes time. The process of changing, renewing, and preparing your mind will not happen overnight, but it *will* happen.

Prayer: Dear Lord, thank you for providing your weapons, armor, strength, and power to equip me to win my battle of the bulge. Forgive me for neglecting to put them on and use them in the area of weight loss. Help me now as I strive to be daily obedient to you in what I eat and how I exercise my body. I commit to spend time in prayer and reading your Word. In Jesus' name, I pray. Amen.

Memory Verse: *"For though we live in the world, we do not wage war as the world does. The weapons we fight with are not the weapons of the world. On the contrary, they have divine power to demolish strongholds. We demolish arguments and every pretension that sets itself up against the knowledge of God, and we take captive every thought to make it obedient to Christ." 2 Corinthians 10:3-5*

Food for Thought

Have you been a Christian for years, but struggle to make your daily Bible reading interesting and applicable? There are numerous devotional books at your local Christian bookstore that will help you get started. In our battle groups, many have found the verses and questions in the *Planning for the Battle of the Bulge* companion workbook/journal to be helpful. Whatever plan you choose, the Word of God is a valuable resource not to be ignored.

Perhaps you are a new believer and have never considered setting aside a portion of each day to read and meditate on God's Word, and you have no idea where to begin. In the Old Testament (the first portion of the Bible) Genesis, Psalms, and Proverbs are good places to start, and in the New Testament (the second portion of the Bible) the books of John, Philippians, and Colossians are practical and easy to understand. Begin by setting aside a few minutes each day to spend in prayer and reading and memorizing portions of God's Word.

DEVELOPING GODLY CHARACTER

"I beseech you therefore, brethren, by the mercies of God, that you present your bodies a living sacrifice, holy, acceptable to God, which is your reasonable service. And do not be conformed to this world, but be transformed by the renewing of your mind, that you may prove what is that good and acceptable and perfect will of God."
Romans 12:1-2

Chapter Ten

Developing Godly Character

I have a dream. I've had this dream since I was in high school. It's not a dream I have when I sleep, one over which I have no control; it's a dream I have when I'm wide-awake. The substance of my dream varies little, though I occasionally add defining details. What is my dream? It is to buy and renovate a two-story Victorian house.

My dream home has a wrap-around porch where I sit in the morning during my quiet time with the Lord. In the evenings, Bill and I sit on the porch swing, watch the sunset, and talk about the day's events.

My house is a true "painted lady," boasting coordinating pastel shades of paint that make the gingerbread and scrollwork trim come alive. It is truly a tribute to the designer and builder. A white picket fence borders the yard—a yard carpeted with freshly mown grass. The garden is a vast sea of flowers displaying more colors than an artist's palette. It's a place where I can walk and talk with God.

The inside of my dream home is as splendid as the outside. The waxed wood floor in the foyer welcomes visitors as they gaze in awe at the high molded ceilings, stained-glass windows, and other decorative details. The winding oak staircase leads to bedrooms filled with antique furniture; handmade quilts grace each bed. Fresh baked bread sends a delightful aroma throughout the house, beckoning one and all to a tasting party at the well-worn oak kitchen table.

A turret is gracefully fitted at one front corner of the house and contains a lovely circular room—my quiet refuge. It is where I retreat to read or write or simply reflect. The telephone doesn't ring in that room, and my family knows not to disturb me there.

My dream house reflects love, care, planning, time, investment, and hard work, and it is more than just beautiful on the outside. While renovating the structure, extra care was taken that the foundation was sure, the structure was stable, and the plumbing and electrical were brought up to code. The house was gutted to make it not only lovely on the outside, but also stable and secure on the inside.

There are two ways to make an old house look as glorious as my dream home. The first is to make superficial repairs and give it a thorough cleaning and a fresh coat of paint. The second is to check the electrical and plumbing; examine for wood rot and termites; and inspect the roof, siding, and foundation, thereby determining what internal improvements need to be made. When all the repairs are complete, then it's time to paint, clean, stain, varnish, and decorate.

A cursory glance may not reveal much difference between the two methods, but the long-term results will be telling. Before long, the first technique will reveal its weaknesses, but the second will produce long-lasting stability because strength was added to the structure in every area.

My renovated Victorian house is only a fantasy, but my dream reminds me of the renovation God wants to do in us as he builds character into our lives. He wants to *gut* us by taking away all that is potentially destructive to our lives. He wants to rebuild us from the inside out with his own godly character so our lives will reflect and glorify him.

After thirty years of yo-yo dieting, I realized that I was making only superficial changes in my eating habits. I was not making the enduring internal renovations in my thinking and character that would result in outward behavioral changes. The results, therefore, were weak, temporary, and potentially destructive to my health. My weight constantly fluctuated, and I never seemed to reach my goal weight and maintain it. I at last saw and accepted myself for what and who I really was—undisciplined, unfocused, impatient, and without self-control. Simply put, I lacked character in the area of my eating habits. Just as a poorly renovated house might have leaks in the plumbing and shorts in the electrical system, I had *leaks* and *shorts* in my character.

Conformed or Transformed

The Scripture verses that opened this chapter are two of my favorites. "I beseech you therefore, brethren, by the mercies of God, that you present your bodies a living sacrifice, holy, acceptable to God, which is your reasonable service. And do not be conformed to this world, but be transformed by the renewing of your mind, that you may prove what is that good and acceptable and perfect will of God" (Romans 12:1-2, emphasis mine). When a sacrifice is laid on an altar, total control is transferred to another. God wants you to *willingly* present yourself to him as a living sacrifice, giving him the control, or the authority, over your body, mind, emotions, and will. He wants you to trust him to transform you from the inside out. It is the difference between submitting to a person (God) and submitting to a program (diet).

One of my Bible college professors used to say, "The problem with a living sacrifice is that it keeps crawling off the altar." That is the perfect description of yo-yo dieters. They make a commitment to a diet, and the minute they become discouraged or bored, they quit. They prefer the quick fix rather than the long-term commitment of sacrificial obedience. They are not willing to submit to God's plan and to refrain from foods that are destructive to their bodies.

Some people do not like the idea of *submitting*, and they recoil at the sound of that word. But, the truth is we all submit every day; it's simply a matter of deciding to what you will submit. When you drive, you submit to traffic laws. When you go to work, you submit to a boss. When you go to school, you submit to a teacher. When you are a member of a sports team, you submit to a coach. When you overeat, you submit to food and your self-indulgence. You choose to whom or to what you will submit.

Romans 12:2 says not to be *conformed* to the world, yet compulsive dieters are constantly subjecting themselves to all that society offers—fad diets, appetite suppressants, fast foods, prepackaged foods, artificial sweeteners and flavorings, super-sized meals, and a busy yet inactive lifestyle. Many dieters conform to the Hollywood standard of physical appearance, and instead of conforming to planning and preparing a healthy menu and exercise program, they waste time and energy dreaming about a fantasy body that is unachievable.

Verse two also says you are to be *transformed*. The word used here means to *metamorphose*, like a caterpillar making the transition into a butterfly. You do that by *renewing*, or renovating, your mind. Sometimes, like the electrical system in an old house, your thinking needs to be "rewired" so your behavior will make a total transformation. Are you trapped in the stage somewhere between a caterpillar and a butterfly? Do you want to become a butterfly, but find you are resisting the changes necessary to allow you to emerge from the cocoon victoriously transformed? Placing yourself sacrificially on God's altar and *remaining there* is the only way to permanently transform your life. God will not force you onto the altar; he asks you to go willingly. He will not force changes in your thinking and behavior; he asks you to do it willingly. God will discipline and nudge you toward obedience, but he will not force you (Hebrews 12:3-11). His army has no draftees; it is composed entirely of volunteers.

As you seek God's direction in the transformation process, you can find help in two prayers the Apostle Paul presented on behalf of the churches at Ephesus (Ephesians 1:15-21) and Colosse (Colossians 1:9-14). Paul's desire for them is exactly what God is longing to do for you in your weight battle.

Paul requested for them:

- That they would have a spirit of *wisdom* and a *knowledge* of God—Ephesians 1:17 and Colossians 1:9
- That their eyes of *understanding* would be enlightened—Ephesians 1:18
- That they would know God's *calling* and the *riches* of his inheritance—Eph. 1:18

- That they would know the greatness of God's *power* toward other believers—Ephesians 1:19 and 20
- That they would know God's *power is greater* than any other (even Satan's)—Ephesians 1:21 and Colossians 1:13
- That they would *walk worthy* of the Lord and please him—Colossians 1:10
- That they would be *strengthened* in the Lord's might—Colossians 1:11
- That they would have *patience* and *longsuffering* with *joy*—Colossians 1:11
- That they would be *thankful*—Colossians 1:12

The word *walk* (Colossians 1:10) implies taking steps like in a journey. Winning the battle of the bulge is a journey; it is a process just as the caterpillar changing into a butterfly. The process consists of daily steps of obedience while building godly character into your life. *Your obedience will build character, and character will win battles.*

Vikki and I didn't even try to lose weight during our first few meetings. We devoted our time to prayer and preparing a battle plan, and worked on developing the character qualities we needed to develop to be effective warriors. The first week we both chose to work on our discipline. Then, as we began each day with discipline in mind, we asked God to strengthen us with his power and to give us his wisdom and knowledge, to understand him and better represent him, and to be patient and pleasing to him in all we did. We prayed what Paul had written to the churches at Ephesus and Colosse, and the process literally transformed our lives as we renovated our thinking.

Working on a new character quality each week was exciting. God was shifting our focus from food to obedience, and we were no longer obsessed with what we were going to eat for our next snack or meal. We determined to eat healthy foods, smaller portions, and maintain regular exercise. As our thinking changed, our behavior changed, and week-by-week the pounds began to drop. God was truly renewing our minds.

Our Weakness Becomes God's Strength

God is fully aware of your struggles and weaknesses, and rather than condemn you, he wants to show his strength through you. He says, "...My grace is sufficient for you, for my power is made perfect in weakness." Thus the Apostle Paul responds, "Therefore I will boast all the more gladly about my weaknesses, so that Christ's power may rest on me. That is why, for Christ's sake, I delight in weaknesses, in insults, in hardships, in persecutions, in difficulties. *For when I am weak, then I am strong*" (2 Corinthians 12:9-10).

When it came to dieting I had numerous weaknesses, but the Lord wanted to take those weaknesses and turn them into strengths. For every failing in me, I found victorious strength in him.

- I was *fearful* of failing once again, but he gave me *courage* (Joshua 1:9).
- I *wavered* in my dieting efforts, but he gave me *perseverance* (2 Peter 1:6).
- I was *confused* about the direction I should take, but he gave me *wisdom* and *direction* (Proverbs 3:5-7).
- I felt *guilty* about my past failures, but he was *merciful* and *forgiving* (Psalm 145:8-9).
- I had a *proud* heart, but he graciously showed me how to be *humble* (1 Peter 5:5b-6).
- I *doubted* that I could succeed, but I found *faithfulness* in him (1 Peter 4:19).
- I was *anxious* about the future, but he taught me *patience* (James 1:2-3).
- I was *lazy* when it came to planning and preparing healthy meals, but he taught me to be *diligent* (Proverbs 12:27).
- I was consumed with *sadness* when I failed, but he filled my heart with *joy* (Nehemiah 8:10b).
- I allowed myself to be *deceived* by the lies of the enemy, but he is *truth* and all that is *honest* (John 14:6).
- I was *dissatisfied* with myself, but he made me *content* in himself (Philippians 4:11).
- My heart was filled with *conflict*, but he gave me *peace* (Philippians 4:7).
- I wallowed in *defeat*, but he gave *victory* (1 Corinthians 15:57-58)!

Renovation Takes Time

My weekly battle groups are filled with Christians who have miserably failed at dieting, and they don't understand why. The nearly universal frustration is, "Sometimes I don't feel like a very good Christian. Why am I disciplined and self-controlled in some areas of my life, but I just can't seem to apply it in the area of my eating?"

The answer is because we take time to develop character qualities and godly attributes in some areas of our lives, but not in our eating. We want the speedy results achieved from fleeting behavioral changes (diets), rather than the lasting effects of a deliberate growth in character and self-discipline. We are self-indulgent, impatient for results, and lacking in perseverance, and the results are disappointment, self-condemnation, and defeat. *Renovation takes time.*

I thought back to some of the positive achievements in my life, and I saw the results of planning and preparation. I realized I was a good student because I disciplined myself to study and do my assignments, and I exercised self-control by not allowing television and other things to distract me. I crafted quality clothing because I patiently honed my sewing skills over a period of many years. I was successful as a children's church instructor and Sunday School teacher because I committed hundreds, if not thousands, of hours to planning and preparation. But, I had never committed to developing those same godly attributes to my eating habits *before* I began a diet. How much more successful I would have been if I had developed patience, determination, and self-control first. *Renovation takes time.*

Do you see *it's not just about the weight*? It's about building godly character into your life through daily obedience. It's about standing together with other Christians as you battle together. It's about representing your heavenly Father so others will place their faith in him. Can you picture yourself as a soldier fighting your battle of the bulge clothed with Christ's character, using his weapons, battling in his strength? Would the outcome of your battle be different? The answer is a resounding *yes!*

So, you've experienced defeats in the past? What are you going to do about your future?

Prayer: Dear Lord, I recognize that there are areas in my life that need to be renovated in order for me to have victory in my battle of the bulge. I now willingly place myself on your altar. If I crawl off, please discipline and nudge me until I get back to where you want me to be. Forgive me for the times I have conformed my thinking and behavior to the world's standards. Help me as I transform my mind and conform my thinking and character to be like Christ's. I want my life to be a tribute to you, my Designer and Builder. In Jesus' name, I pray. Amen.

Memory Verse: *"I beseech you therefore, brethren, by the mercies of God, that you present your bodies a living sacrifice, holy, acceptable to God, which is your reasonable service. And do not be conformed to this world, but be transformed by the renewing of your mind, that you may prove what is that good and acceptable and perfect will of God."* *Romans 12:1-2*

Food for Thought

Fad diets reveal lack of character. They show you the areas in which you need to grow and become more like Christ. Below is a list of character qualities. Beside each one, note how you can develop and apply it to your battle. For example, you might **discipline** yourself to keep a record of all the foods you eat and complete your *Planning for the Battle of the Bulge* companion workbook/journal each day. You may exercise **self-control** by limiting your portion size. You might take **responsibility** for your actions rather than blame your circumstances or another person. You might exercise **patience** in reaching your goals. You may add others to the list if you wish.

Discipline:

Diligence:

Patience:

Self-control:

Faithfulness:

Vigilance:

Discernment:

Responsibility:

Obedience:

Dependability:

Integrity:

Orderliness:

Honesty:

Perseverance:

Humility:

Decisiveness:

Contentment:

Loyalty:

Love:

Joy:

Compassion:

Focus:

Accountability:

GIVING GOD THE GLORY

*"So whether you eat or drink or whatever you
do, do it all for the glory of God."*
1 Corinthians 10:31

CHAPTER ELEVEN

Giving God the Glory

Rich golds, refreshing blues, and leafy greens shone across the expanse of the cool tile floor, while tiny rainbows danced on the adjacent walls.

I sat at the kitchen table, feet nestled beneath me, sipping a steaming cup of coffee, and staring with satisfaction and contentment down the hallway to our front entrance. A day earlier, Bill had installed a magnificent eighteen-by-seventy-two-inch stained-glass window in the sidelight of our front door.

The scene depicted a large peacock, tail flowing and head turned majestically over his shoulder. The background was of gold glass, and the entire window was outlined with clear bevels, producing the rainbow effect on the walls, ceiling, and floor. I don't think a single person passed through that door without commenting on the loveliness of that window.

I spent many mornings sitting in that same spot, sipping coffee and staring down the hall as God's sunlight made the colors in that window come alive. It was a wonderful spot to pray and read my Bible.

Now, let me tell you the rest of the story. I made that beautiful window. Yes, *me*! Even my friends who knew I had taken a class in stained glass were amazed at the finished product. I studied nine weeks in the class; spent hundreds of dollars on tools, glass, and other supplies; honed my skills on other projects for a year; and then spent three months creating my window. I cut each of the hundreds of pieces of glass by hand, ground them with a diamond grinder, foiled them in copper, and then soldered them together. It's the most beautiful piece of stained glass I ever made.

I don't tell you this story to boast about my art skills and the beauty of my window, but rather to boast about my *Lord's* creativity and magnificence. I'm proud of that window, and I suppose I could take full credit for my workmanship, but the truth is, I am creative because *he* is creative, and *he* created me in *his* image. *He* designed the colors in my window, and they dance on my tile floor because *he* created sunlight. *He* gave me the ability and desire to work with my hands. *He* created the majestic peacock that could be copied into glass and later enjoyed while sipping a cup of coffee. *He* is awesome!

Even a stained-glass window can bring glory to God when seen in the proper perspective. Yet it's not the window itself, but *the creative process that brings him glory*. It's how I use my time, my mind, and my skills to create beauty. And you—*yes, you*—are a beautiful creation of his workmanship. "For we are God's workmanship, created in Christ Jesus to do good works, which God prepared in advance for us to do" (Ephesians 2:10).

And so it is with weight loss. It's not just the end result, the achieved goal, the weight lost—it's the *process* of a changed heart and a changed mind and the day by day obedience that brings glory to God. *It's not just about the weight.*

Created to Praise

I've gained and lost hundreds of pounds over the past thirty years. I've actually reached my goal two or three times, and been within sight of it countless others. When I reached my goal or came close, I was always immensely proud of *my* success. I didn't exactly flaunt it, but I loved it when someone noticed what *I* had accomplished. There was nothing wrong with feeling good about my weight loss and having pride in my accomplishment, but I was missing the bigger picture—*I have been created to praise God, and I exist to give him glory in everything I do.*

I liken my years of yo-yo dieting to looking at my stained-glass window while it was still lying on the plywood workbench. The glass was cut and pieced together with skill and precision, and it had potential beauty, but it did not reveal its true magnificence until it was placed in front of sunlight. I had potential too, but until I placed myself and my weight-loss efforts before the Lord and allowed him to shine through my life it was all about me—*my* pride, *my* looks, *my* accomplishments. Just as artificial light does not create as vibrant an effect as natural light, my feeble attempts at weight loss produced temporary, artificial results.

I shared earlier how I decided not to tell anyone about my battle of the bulge. I knew, however, the time would come when people would notice my weight loss and begin to ask questions. I was anxious that I wouldn't be able to adequately articulate what was happening in my life, and that I wouldn't know how to give praise where it was due. But I need not have worried, for I soon had several opportunities to share about the process and give glory where it was due.

Our youngest son, Jonathan, noticed my weight loss and was very encouraging during my first few months of battling. I think he was surprised (and relieved) that I wasn't talking nonstop about dieting, as usual. Instead, I shared with him the reasons for my victory and the course of action I was taking.

One day in October, Jonathan came home from football practice and announced he was quitting the team. "Coach hates me," he said. "I'm through with football."

I refrained from reminding Jonathan that we never allowed them to quit a team once they were committed, but I could tell he was really upset and decided to bring it up later if necessary.

"Tell me, why do you think your coach hates you?" I asked.

"He yells at me all the time and never tells me I do a good job. I haven't missed kicking an extra point all season, but he never says anything good to me. I don't care any more. I quit!"

I knew Jonathan's coach didn't hate him. It's true, the coach could be rough on the boys, and his vocabulary could be loud and coarse, but he liked the boys and tried, in his own way, to motivate them.

I didn't want Jonathan to be miserable for the rest of the season, but I also knew giving up wasn't the answer. Besides, it was his senior year of high school, and I knew he would forever regret his decision. I tried to encourage him with, *I know he really likes you; the team needs you; playoffs are about to begin; it doesn't matter if people comment on your performance because you know you're doing your best.* It didn't work!

Finally, I said, "Jonathan, who is your enemy?"

"Coach!" he retorted immediately, flashing me a satisfied grin.

"Jonathan, I mean it," I said seriously. "Who is your enemy in this situation?"

Jonathan knew enough about my weight-loss program to know exactly what I was talking about. "Satan," he said. "Satan is my enemy."

"Okay, think about it. What does he want to accomplish in your life in regard to this decision?"

After a moment, Jonathan replied, "Well, he wants me to quit the team."

"Right," I said. "You're one of the best kickers this school has ever had and, if you quit, you'll be letting down the team and the school. What else?"

"I would be a poor Christian testimony to the guys and Coach, I guess."

"All right," I said, "what do you think God wants to accomplish in your life through this situation?"

"Well, he doesn't want me to quit. He wants me to be patient and stick with it." He thought for a moment and added, "He wants me to try my best, no matter what, and he wants me to do what Coach says even when he yells at me."

Jonathan didn't quit the football team and went on to a perfect season in extra points kicked. But more than that, he recognized that *people* are not his enemies. He learned that through the process of obedience and growth, he can give God the glory in every situation.

As I shed more weight it became noticeable to my friends, and one day my friend Sharon approached me. "I can see you've lost weight, and it looks good, but there is something different about you. It's more than just the weight. You're walking taller and straighter and your whole countenance is more joyful and content." Then, she asked the inevitable question: "What are you doing?"

The difference Sharon saw was the result of my new focus on obedience. She saw that my outlook was different from the other times I had tried to lose weight. I wasn't focused on food or a specific diet plan; each time I was confronted with food, I focused on the process of building godly character through daily obedience. I wasn't announcing a diet or boasting about the weight. Christ's spiritual light was shining through the window of my life just as his sunlight shone through my stained-glass window.

I told Sharon about our weekly battle group, and because she only needed to lose a few pounds, I wasn't sure she'd be interested. The next week she began to meet with us and, though she lost fifteen pounds, she continued in the Bible study for three years. Why? Because Sharon understood *it isn't just about the weight.*

My husband noticed my clothes were looser, and I was pleased when he asked if I was losing weight.

I simply said, "Yes, I've lost a few pounds."

"Well," Bill persisted, "what are you doing?"

I was somewhat defensive as I asked, "Do you really want to know, or are you just asking?"

I was apprehensive as I told my pastor husband about boot camp, enlistment, battle plans, and the enemy. I assumed he would think it was silly, but he quietly sat and listened. When I finished, he looked at me thoughtfully, and said, "You know, I could really use those concepts in my counseling, especially with couples. When couples are having marriage problems, they usually view their spouse as the enemy. If they could realize that Satan is the enemy and wants to destroy their marriage, they could focus on solving their problems instead of focusing on the faults of the other person."

He put something into words that was becoming clearer to me daily. *These same principles could be applied in every area of our lives and in every battle.*

"Yes," I said, "if couples could see themselves as soldiers in God's army, together fighting a common enemy with common weapons for a common cause, they could resolve personal conflict without attacking each other. And, God would get the glory through the process of marriages being restored."

My friends and family were beginning to see that *it isn't just about the weight.* I didn't have to worry about God getting the glory; it was happening as a natural result of my obedience to him.

God's Gift of Food

Food, appetite, and weight control may seem like an insignificant area for a spiritual battle, but as we saw in the beginning of the chapter, "…whether you eat or drink or *whatever you do, do it all for the glory of God*" (1 Corinthians 10:31, emphasis mine).

Is there anything too small or unimportant to warrant God's attention? If he created you (and he did) and gave you life (and he did), then shouldn't each moment of your life be lived for him?

"For by him all things were created: things in heaven and on earth, visible and invisible, whether thrones or powers or rulers or authorities; *all things were created by him and for him*" (Colossians 1:16, emphasis mine).

"You are worthy, our Lord and God, *to receive glory and honor and power, for you created all things*, and by your will they were created and have their being" (Revelation 4:11, emphasis mine).

Throughout Scripture, food and feasts were occasions for praise and worship. Yet from the beginning, Satan tried to tempt man and distort the marvelous gifts of food and appetite. Food is such a normal part of our lives that we can easily be caught unaware.

God gave you your appetite so he could satisfy it with his gift of food. *What*, you say, *my appetite is a gift?* For most of my life, I viewed my appetite as a curse—something I could not control or satisfy, and I often prayed for God to take it away. But I was trying to satisfy it with the wrong food and too much of it. Bodily hunger is designed to be satisfied with healthy foods in moderate portions. How many times have you tried to appease your hunger by overeating or indulging in foods that are loaded with sugar or other unhealthy ingredients, only to find you're not really satisfied at all? Instead, your stomach is uncomfortably overfilled, you have a headache, you feel guilty, and you're soon craving more food. Over-indulgence doesn't satisfy; it only creates a cycle of wanting more, eating more, and feeling guilty.

As you limit your portions and change your eating habits to include more fresh fruits and vegetables, dairy products, and whole-grain foods, your hunger will be satisfied and your soul will be content. The more you cut back on sugar, fast foods, and prepackaged foods, the less you will desire them, and you will steadily lose weight. Your appetite will be satisfied when you eat the right foods in moderate portions.

Food and appetite are not the only gifts Satan misrepresents. He has distorted and cheapened our sexual desires (appetites). People try to satisfy those God-given desires with multiple partners, sex outside of marriage, and pornography, but they are never content and keep seeking the next person and the next thrill. More is better, they think. But *our sexual appetites can only be satisfied within the boundaries of God's gift of marriage.*

Our souls, too, hunger to be filled. People try religion, donating to charities, supporting humanitarian causes, and other good works. While these are good things to do, *the soul can only be satisfied when it is filled with the gift of the Holy Spirit through faith in Christ.* Satan distorts the gift by saying we must work to receive what is freely given by God.

I recently spoke at a luncheon, and the chairwoman made a profound statement in her opening prayer. She thanked God for the food, and then said, "May these foods do for our bodies what your Son did for our souls." Jesus satisfies our spiritual hunger with his gift of eternal life, he satisfies our physical hunger with his gift of healthy food, and he satisfies our sexual appetites with his gift of marriage.

No matter what the hunger, *God-given appetites can only be satisfied with God-given gifts.* And *that* is when he gets the glory!

Worship during Meals

Jewish feasts set the pattern for worship during meals. They were joyous occasions of celebration, and great care was taken in choosing and preparing the food. The Passover, the Feast of Trumpets (Rosh Hashanah), the Day of Atonement (Yom Kippur), and the Feast of Tabernacles were times to enjoy food and festivities, but the focus was always to be on worship, praise, fellowship, and remembrance of God's provision, protection, and presence.

Meals in our culture have become something we rush through on the way to our next meeting, sporting event, school activity, or church function. Families eat in shifts and can't remember the last time they sat down to a leisurely meal together. Menus consist of frozen, canned, or prepackaged meals, sugared snacks, greasy chips, and other heavily preserved foods.

Understandably, most of us have busy lives, but why not consider making at least one meal each week a 'feast'—a time to develop an attitude of worship, praise, gratitude, and service.

It's no accident that the Bible records so many events around food, for our meals were intended to have purpose. Consider the following:

- Food is to nourish our bodies that we may fulfill our purpose on earth and to give us strength to work to provide for our families, serve in our churches and communities, and keep our bodies healthy.
- Food is designed to be a pleasurable gift.
- Meals are for fellowship, a time for sharing joys and concerns, mentoring friends

and loved ones, and teaching children.

- Meals are a time of physical rest from work, as well as mental and emotional rest from the concerns and troubles of the day.
- Providing food for others is a way to help the needy, thereby verifying God's Word as truth.
- Meals are a time to build character such as self-control, discipline, gratefulness, sharing, and contentment.
- Meals are a time of praise and thanksgiving for provision, creation, and blessings.
- Preparing the meal is a time to prepare our hearts for worship, while cleaning up after the meal is an act of serving others.
- Meals are a time to entertain guests and show hospitality.

Our meals may not be as symbolic as the feasts of Israel, but they should be a time to focus on the Lord and all he has done for us.

Prayer: Dear Lord, please help me as I purpose to give you praise, worship, and glory through the process of learning to be obedient to you in my eating habits. I pray that your light would shine through my life. Thank you for your marvelous gift of food. Thank you for the variety, the taste, and the bounty of your creation. Forgive me when I take it for granted. Help me to make my meals a time to worship you. In Jesus' name, I pray. Amen.

Memory Verse: *"So whether you eat or drink or whatever you do, do it all for the glory of God."* *1 Corinthians 10:31*

Food for Thought

Here are a few suggestions to help make your next meal more memorable.

- Take turns asking God's blessing on your meal. Memorized prayers are nice, but speak from your heart.
- *Don't* watch TV during your meals. Your mind is occupied with the programming, and you are being robbed of the precious gifts of family, food, fellowship, and worship.
- Ask each person to tell something special about his or her day; it will give you a listening heart.

- Ask each person to give praise for one thing; it will give you a worshipful heart.
- Share prayer requests; it will give you a compassionate heart.
- Make cleanup a family affair; it will give you a servant's heart.
- Thank those who prepared the meal; it will give you a grateful heart.
- Thank those who provided the finances to buy the food; it will give you an understanding heart.

CHAPTER TWELVE

LOOKING YOUR BEST
FROM THE INSIDE OUT

"For you created my inmost being, you knit me together in my mother's womb. I praise you because I am fearfully and wonderfully made; your works are wonderful, I know that full well. My frame was not hidden from you when I was made in the secret place. When I was woven together in the depths of the earth, your eyes saw my unformed body. All the days ordained for me were written in your book before one of them came to be."
Psalm 139:13-16

CHAPTER TWELVE

Looking Your Best from the Inside Out

PART 1

"Mary," Carol called in a hushed voice.

I looked up from the knick-knacks I was studying and glanced around the antiques store. Carol was standing in front of a large glass case filled with porcelain, silver, and other items too valuable to leave in the open. She had a grin on her face, and I knew she'd found a special treasure.

"Mary," she repeated, beckoning with her finger, "over here."

I loved going to antiques stores and auctions with Carol. We could shop for hours and not buy a thing, or come home with a carload of treasures with barely enough room for us to squeeze into the vehicle. I walked across the store to see what treasure she had found.

"Look," she said. I followed her gaze to a black basalt teapot, creamer, and sugar combination. "It's exactly like your set."

She was right. The raised white figures set on black porcelain identified the set as being made by the Josiah Wedgwood Company and it was exactly like my service.

"It's beautiful, isn't it?" I murmured.

Carol knows I have a weakness for anything made by Wedgwood. I have several pieces of the traditional raised white on blue and a family set of dinnerware, but the black basalt teapot set is my favorite. It's a double treasure because it belonged to my husband's family, and was given to me by my mother-in-law.

"Yes, but look. Look at the price tag," she said excitedly.

I twisted my neck to look at the tiny paper tag. Eight hundred and fifty dollars!

"Oh, oh" I stuttered. "Oh, my!"

"Did you have any idea it was worth so much?" Carol asked.

"No, I didn't." I was dumbfounded.

I probably don't need to tell you that I cherished both my tea set and my mother-in-law's sacrificial giving even more than I had before. My tea set was carefully displayed in a glass-fronted cabinet, and I knew it had value, but I now had a renewed appreciation for its beauty and worth.

Discovering Our Value

I've always had a deep appreciation for *life*, especially since I survived a rare form of cancer as an infant, but I can't say I've always been genuinely grateful for my *body*. I didn't always like its size, shape, and color—my hair was too curly, my face too freckled, my legs too long, and my skin too light. And, I felt God should have been more equitable when it came to passing out certain body parts.

In elementary school I was the tallest girl in my class, so I slouched and developed poor posture. Someone once pointed out my knocked knees, and I became self-conscious about the way I walked. Boys teased me about my pudgy, underdeveloped figure, and I felt unfeminine. Others pointed out the constellation of freckles on my face, my stubby nose, and full lips. I was hurt by these comments, and I became self-conscious about my appearance. I entered my twenties with a list of so-called "imperfect" body parts that would have made a plastic surgeon wealthy.

It didn't start out that way. When I was a little girl, I believed my father when he told me I was more beautiful than Elizabeth Taylor who at that time was considered the most beautiful woman in the world. I know he didn't mean to damage my self-esteem, but it didn't take me long to figure out that his comment was just a father's loving opinion. Comments like that were programming me to measure myself against an idealistic yardstick, and I hadn't even reached junior high school and the inevitable locker room comparisons.

Accepting Unchangeable Physical Features

Many of our physical features can be easily enhanced or changed apart from the dangers and expense of reconstructive or plastic surgery. Hair color can be changed with dye, teeth can be whitened with gels or straightened with braces, blemishes can be covered with makeup, and our muscles can be toned with exercise and proper nutrition. But what about those physical features that are unchangeable? Let's examine how we might look at our bodies from a more positive view.

Don't compare yourself with others. It's a waste of your time and energy. Measuring yourself against others will either make you feel temporarily euphoric or keep you constantly depressed. There will always be someone prettier, more handsome, stronger, or thinner. It's unrealistic to strive to be the most attractive person among your associates. The Bible says we're foolish if we make comparisons. "For we dare not class ourselves or compare ourselves with those who commend themselves. But they, measuring themselves by themselves, and comparing themselves among themselves, *are* *not wise"* (2 Corinthians 10:12, emphasis mine).

Don't view yourself through the world's eyes. The world's view of beauty changes as quickly as the latest fashions. When I was a young girl, women with rounded figures were considered the most appealing, but it wasn't long before rail-thin Twiggy was the rage. Be neat and clean and choose your clothing and hairstyle wisely, but don't try to live up to an impossible standard set by fashion marketers. The ultimate fashion designer created you, and his design never goes out of style! "Do nothing out of selfish ambition or vain conceit…" (Philippians 2:3).

View yourself through the eyes of your Creator. If you have accepted Christ as Savior, the Bible says you are indwelled with and sealed by the Holy Spirit (Ephesians 1:13). If the very God of the universe has chosen to live within you, you are obviously of great value to him.

In 1979, actors Dudley Moore and Bo Derek starred in a movie called *10*. In the story, Moore's character views Derek as having a perfect face and figure, hence the reference to the phrase "She's a   perfect 10."

One evening, I was speaking to a large group of ladies from ages eighteen to eighty. I asked how many thought they had a perfect body, and I was not surprised when not one hand was raised. I continued by saying *I* have a perfect body. Understandably, there were a lot of snickers and even some outright laughter!

I went on to say that my arms can hug, and my ears can listen to a broken heart and hear a bird sing. My tongue can encourage others, share the gospel of Christ, and sing praises. My eyes can view God's creation, and my heart can praise him. My breasts have nursed three babies, and my legs and feet can carry me where I want to go. *I am a perfect 10!*

I asked the ladies again how many thought they had a perfect body and, in a room now void of laughter, nearly every hand was raised.

Give praise and thanksgiving for your body, and accept your unchangeable features as a gift from God.

My brother David has cerebral palsy; he wears a leg brace and walks with a limp. As you can imagine, life has been more of a challenge for David than the average person. He started school a couple of years after the other kids his age, and he had to make an extra effort with his studies. He was always "it" longer than anyone else when we played tag, and I don't remember David ever winning a neighborhood foot race.

My brother experienced numerous other hardships, and I've seen him weep in frustration. But I've *never* heard David complain about his handicap—*not even once*. If anything, he's used his struggles as an example to encourage others. For years, he refused to use a handicap-parking sticker, though he was certainly entitled. He works hard at his job as a food supervisor (in a state penitentiary, no less), is active in his church, and is a wonderful husband and father of three.

David has accepted his unchangeable features as a gift from God. I think he would say he is a perfect 10!

When I view myself by the world's standards, I might be able to appreciate some of my features, but I will eventually come up short. When I turn my eyes to look into the glass case of Scripture and see the price tag God has placed on me, I have unspeakable value and beauty. *I am priceless!*

Instituting a Spirit of Gratefulness

Have you ever spent time carefully choosing a gift for someone, but when you gave it to them your present was not met with the enthusiasm and appreciation you expected? I wonder if that's how God feels when we grumble about our "inferior" body parts. It must be like a slap in the face—like telling him he didn't know what he was doing when he created us. How very pleased the enemy must be when we express dissatisfaction with our bodies; he has won another victory.

Perhaps you've never considered that dissatisfaction with your unchangeable physical features is really placing blame on God, but it is precisely that. It also reveals a lack of trust that God knew exactly what he was doing and had your best interest at heart, when he created you. Perhaps you've had an accident that has permanently scarred or handicapped you; perhaps ill health has encumbered you in some way. God knew what he was doing when he allowed those things to happen.

Consider what the Scriptures say.

Job 10:8—God intricately made and fashioned you.

Job 10:11—He clothed you with skin and flesh in your mother's womb.

Job 10:12—He gave you life and knit you together with bones and sinews.

Psalm 139:14—You are fearfully and wonderfully made.

Matthew 6:26—You are valuable.

John 3:16—He loves you so much he sent his Son to die for your sins.

I Peter 1:18—You are so precious he chose to redeem you.

Hebrews 4:15—He understands and sympathizes with your weaknesses.

Psalm 119:75—He allows affliction in his faithfulness.

Understanding and accepting the value and the gift of your physical body is vital to your battle. How effective would an army be if its soldiers constantly questioned their superior officers' wisdom and purposes? How could they have unity among the troops?

How could they make a prepared defense against the enemy?

Accepting who you are and how God made you is *your choice*. It is *your choice* to use your body to serve and to glorify him.

Prayer: "Heavenly Father, I'm gaining a better understanding of the value you place on my physical body. Please forgive me for the times I've complained about my unchangeable physical features. I accept them as a gift from you, and I desire to honor and praise you with every part of my being. If I revert to my former way of thinking, remind me to examine your Word and view myself again through your eyes. In Jesus' name, I pray. Amen."

PART 2

Teapots and Temples

I have a collection of teapots, mostly gifts from friends and relatives. I can tell you who gave each one to me, and the story behind the gift. Some are more attractive than others, but I can make tea in each one. Some hold one cup of tea, and some hold four cups. Some can be put in the dishwasher or microwave, and others must be hand-washed and dried. Some are used more often than others, and each one is uniquely displayed.

When people look at my teapots, they usually point to a particular one, and say, "Oh, I really like that one." Each teapot is exceptional in size, shape, and color; and I love them all. But, what really matters is that whether they are appraised by a temporal value system at eight hundred and fifty dollars or eight dollars and fifty cents, they are all teapots, they all make tea, and they all need care.

Each person on earth is a unique creation too. We each look different, and we come in all sizes, shapes, and colors. Some may be more attractive than others, but we each need special care, and we all have the same purpose—that we might "be to the praise of his glory" (Ephesians 1:14).

During Old Testament times, the tabernacle (and later the temple) was a visible sign that God was present among his people. After Christ died and ascended into heaven, he sent his Holy Spirit to dwell within those who placed their faith in Christ as Savior. When Paul wrote to the Corinthians using the word picture that the body is the temple of the Holy Spirit, he knew they would grasp the spiritual significance of living a holy and pure life, inside and outside. The temple was a visual representation of who God is, and he gave specific instructions for its construction and maintenance. It was a place of purity, sacrifice, holiness, and honor.

In like manner, God gives us instruction for our conduct, because we are his visual representatives to the world. Our lives and our bodies should be vessels of purity, sacrifice, holiness, and honor. Just as it is important for us to keep our lives and minds pure, and our spirits fed on his Word, it is also important for us to maintain our physical temples (bodies) with healthy food and exercise. We are much more productive when our bodies are fit.

Maintaining the Temple

Our outward appearance is an expression of what and who we are inwardly. Our faces reflect inward joy or sorrow. Our clothing reflects whether we take time to carefully choose, wash and iron our garments. With the exception of medical problems and eating disorders, our weight reflects whether we have discipline and self-control in our eating.

I once knew a gentleman who was a sad example of a Christian. He and his wife struggled to keep their weight under control, but there was a vast difference between them. Her hair was well coiffed, her makeup was neatly applied and her clothes were stylish, clean, and in good taste. She had a servant's heart and would do anything to help another. Her husband, on the other hand, wore rumpled clothing that was fifteen years out of style, barely combed his hair, often had body odor, and exhibited behavior that was self-centered and offensive. Sadly, people left the church because of him.

The Gospel of Jesus Christ is the greatest message in the world. Tragically, many people will reject that message, but *no one should ever reject Christ because they were adversely affected by our behavior or physical appearance.*

Some people feel how we look physically is irrelevant; they say the message of the gospel is all that matters. Unfortunately, the messenger also matters. God has chosen *people* to get his message out, and before we ever have the opportunity to open our mouths and speak, our overall outward appearance will already have given a positive or negative impression. Whether we like it or not, people will judge our faith by how we look.

That's not right, you say, *they need to get to know the real me before they make a judgment.* That would be nice, but you cannot get away from first impressions. Reasonable or not, before people are amused by your wit, charmed by your manners, and impressed with your theological views, they will make assumptions about you, *and your message,* based on your dress, facial expressions, posture, hair, body odor, and yes, even your weight.

Representing the Savior

Soldiers in the U.S. Army represent their homeland, their flag, and their commander in chief. Not only are they expected to abide by the Army code of behavior, but they must maintain a physical appearance that reflects their position.

As a soldier in God's army, you represent your future home in heaven, your banner the cross, and your commander in chief the Lord Jesus Christ. You are expected to abide by the behavioral guidelines in Scripture and take care of your physical body, the temple of the Holy Spirit. Hey, soldier, how are you reflecting your position?

Not only are you a soldier, but you are also an ambassador for Christ (2 Corinthians 5:20). An ambassador represents the king or president, and acts in his place. The foreign nation will make judgments about the ambassador's king and country based on the way the ambassador presents himself. The world will make judgments about God by the way you present yourself.

That verse also says God is pleading *through you* for people to trust Christ as their Savior. What an awesome responsibility! Your words, your actions, your attitudes, and your appearance are being used by God to *plead* with others to come to him for salvation. No one should reject Christ because he was not represented well.

Gifts are wrapped in pretty paper because the gift inside is special. Homes are kept neat and clean because it reflects on the owner. Churches are painted, cleaned, and landscaped to attract people to come inside and hear God's message. As a soldier, an ambassador, and a child of the Almighty God, the King of kings, the Lord of lords, you have the privilege of presenting God's gift of eternal life to the world; it should be presented in the best package possible.

Psalm 70:4 says "…let those who love Your salvation say continually, 'Let God be magnified!'" Your life should magnify the Lord.

The question should not be "What do others think about *me* when they look at me" but rather "What do others think about *Christ* when they look at me?"

Prayer: Dear Lord, thank you for allowing me to represent you to the world. I want to use every part of my being to magnify Christ and present his gift of eternal life to others. Please help me be aware of any areas in my behavior or physical appearance that may be a detriment to your message, and I will commit to make the necessary changes. In Jesus' name, I pray. Amen.

Memory Verse: *"For you created my inmost being, you knit me together in my mother's womb. I praise you because I am fearfully and wonderfully made; your works are wonderful, I know that full well. My frame was not hidden from you when I was made in the secret place. When I was woven together in the depths of the earth, your eyes saw my unformed body. All the days ordained for me were written in your book before one of them came to be." Psalm 139:13-16*

Food for Thought

Periodically, we all need to make changes in our behavior and appearance—that's part of life and growth. Sometimes we don't make those changes because we are lazy, and sometimes we don't make the changes because we are simply unaware.

If you genuinely want to know how your behavior and physical appearance come across to others, ask yourself the following questions, or better yet, ask a close friend who will be loving and honest with you. Be prepared for some surprises and determine not to take offense at his or her suggestions.

- Do my facial expressions show I am friendly, or do I put others off?
- Does my body language say I'm approachable, or does it say *stay away from me*?
- Do I need to update my wardrobe?
- Do my clothes appear rumpled and in need of washing and ironing?
- Are my shoes shined and do they match my clothing?
- Do I need to wear makeup, or do I need to change my makeup in any way?
- Do I need to make changes to my hairstyle or hair color?
- Is my facial hair, or lack thereof, appropriate?
- Is my jewelry appropriate, or is it overdone?
- Am I modest in my behavior and clothing?
- Does my posture need improvement?
- Do I need to lose weight?
- Are there any other areas in which I need to change my attitude or appearance?

SUPPORT FROM THE HOME FRONT

CHAPTER THIRTEEN

Support from the Home Front

PART 1

Although born of noble birth and into privileged class, he left his own country and family to travel thousands of miles by sea to pledge his support to a man he did not know and to a cause that was not his own. He joined the army of this alien nation as a volunteer and took no payment for his services. In fact, he believed so passionately in the cause of this fledgling army that he pledged his personal fortune. It wasn't his country and it wasn't his battle, yet he fought willingly and bravely, and he humbly placed himself under the command of another. He was a remarkable soldier, because he had all the markings of a remarkable man—loyalty, courage, dependability, humility, and more. At only nineteen years of age, he was given the rank of major general.

Notwithstanding his leadership qualities and bravery in battle, perhaps his most vital military role was that of support to his commander in chief. He promoted his commander's interests, gave wise advice, and offered a listening ear and encouraging words. When other officers proved disloyal and tried to have the commander relieved of his duties, this support man warned the leader and steadfastly defended him.

Together, these two men planned military strategies, fought side by side, suffered hunger and exposure, agonized over defeats, and celebrated victories. Though more than twenty years separated them in age, the young volunteer and the military leader established an intimate friendship that lasted until the commander's death.

The young man who played such a vital role in our nation's defense and proved invaluable to his superior was Marie Joseph Paul Yves Roche Gilbert du Motier, better known as the Marquis de Lafayette, aide extraordinaire to General George Washington.

We all need a Lafayette in our lives—someone who understands what we are fighting for, has faith in our cause, and will stand by us in our times of need. We need someone who will be honest, loyal, understanding, and encouraging—someone who will fight alongside us, even if it isn't his or her battle.

Choosing a Support Person

We tend to place great importance on people who are self-made and independent, and, certainly, there is much to be said for those who exhibit these qualities. But there is just as much to be said for teamwork.

I began my battle with the faulty perception that I could make it on my own. (After five years, I still need support and accountability.) But God knew I needed a battle buddy, and it was abundantly clear that Vikki was to be that person. Because we were both engaged in the same war, it was easy to recognize each other's needs and offer encouragement and support. As others joined us, we had the privilege of offering support through our weekly Bible study. Eventually, we established a more structured format that developed into this book and a thirteen-week program designed to support and encourage others.

Ideally, you too will have someone who is fighting his or her own battle of the bulge and together you can join forces. However, if you are in the battle alone, prayerfully ask a friend or loved one to help you in your struggle. *Who you choose will be significant to your future success.*

Ask yourself the following questions as you consider whom you will choose for your support battle buddy.

- Can I can be totally honest and open about my thoughts and feelings with _____?
- Will _____ support me through prayer?
- Does _____ understand the unique difficulties of my battle? (It will be helpful for your battle buddy to read this book.)
- Will _____ be available to receive phone calls and meet with me at least once a week? (Although you will need someone with availability, remember to be considerate of his or her time.)
- Have I adequately expressed what I need and expect in a battle buddy?
- Have I sufficiently explained my unique needs, struggles, goals, and objectives?

Once you've decided upon a support person, make sure your lines of communication are open. Don't expect your battle buddy to read your mind.

Prayer for the Soldier: "Dear Lord, Please give me wisdom as I choose a battle buddy, and help me as I articulate my needs. In return, I pray I will be a positive support to my battle buddy in his or her battles. Thank you for my support person, but may I always remember that you are my ultimate source of strength, comfort, and support. In Jesus' name, I pray. Amen."

PART 2

Guidelines for the Support Battle Buddy

This section is specifically written for you, the person dedicated to supporting the one who has enlisted to fight. In the same way support is shown for the military when our nation is at war, you need to show support for those with personal battles in your home, at church, and at work. "Carry each other's burdens, and in this way you will fulfill the law of Christ" (Galatians 6:2). Weight may not be your personal battle, but you are in the war in the sense that you have agreed to support your friend or loved one. I recommend you read this entire book to get a complete grasp of what your soldier is facing. Hebrews 10:24 tells us to "…consider how we may spur one another on toward love and good deeds." You have the unique opportunity to spur your loved one on to victory.

Remember the old westerns and war movies where the good guy says to his buddy just before running into the line of fire, *Cover me*? As a support battle buddy, you will not be able to fight the battle for your soldier, but you can provide *cover* in several ways. The following suggestions are designed to help you in your role and should be adjusted to fit your specific situation.

- Galatians 5:22 and 23 should be the theme verses for your support role. "But the fruit of the Spirit is love, joy, peace, patience, kindness, goodness, faithfulness, gentleness, self-control." These are characteristics you will need to exhibit toward your loved one.

- Just as *you* are completely accepted by Christ the way you are, *completely* accept your loved one right where he or she is. This will be a long war, and your soldier needs to know your loving support can be depended upon for the duration.

- As much as possible, try to eat the same foods as your soldier. He or she is probably not following a specific diet, but rather trying to make permanent changes in eating habits. Even if you don't need to lose weight, you should be eating healthy food too.

- Consider temporarily removing foods from your home or workplace that may prove an overwhelming temptation. Certain foods can be like a land mine ready to explode.

- Food is not the only battle your loved one is facing. Be aware of other struggles in his or her life.
- Pray together. If you're not comfortable praying aloud, spend a few minutes in silence. Seek God's guidance as to how you can be a good support.
- Verbally express your love and support. Chances are this will be a lifelong war, and continuous verbal affirmation is important.
- Rejoice in all victories, no matter how small. What may seem inconsequential to you could be the encouragement your soldier needs to endure one more day.
- Be understanding of failures, but don't allow your soldier to wallow in defeat. Make constructive suggestions and together devise new battle plans to avoid the same mistakes.
- Consider sharing a meal when you go out to eat. If you're at a self-serve buffet restaurant, offer to get the food for your soldier to help avoid temptation.
- *Don't condemn*! Your soldier has spent more than enough time in self-condemnation and needs positive reinforcement.
- Initially, grocery shopping can be a huge temptation. If your soldier is the primary shopper, offer to go along, or temporarily take on the responsibility yourself.
- If you suspect your loved one is hiding food or has not been honest in some way, *lovingly* confront him or her. *Don't accuse*, but speak the truth in love and assist in determining a solution to the problem.
- Help with food planning and/or preparation. This is a good way to spend time together and allows both parties to have menu input.
- Be observant, and note when your soldier loses weight.
- Eat together, and eat slowly. Make your meal times memorable. (See Chapter 11.)
- Keep your soldier accountable for daily victories and defeats, weekly weight gain and loss, and character development.
- Protect your soldier. Don't allow others to tease or criticize. When someone offers tempting food, help your loved one resist. This is especially important for a young child or adolescent.
- Physical exercise is essential to health and weight-loss efforts, yet it may be one of the biggest battles. If possible, exercise together, even if it begins with a short walk around the block. Be sensitive to your soldier's physical capabilities.

- Be realistic in your expectations and set goals together for weight loss and character development. Your loved one did not gain weight overnight and will not lose it overnight.
- Even if you are not battling your weight, consider sharing one of your other life battles and become mutually accountable.
- Be prepared for setbacks and plateaus in your soldier's weight-loss journey. These can be difficult times for both of you to stay focused.

Some Verbal Do's and Don'ts

Remember the pain you felt as a child when someone made fun of you or called you a cruel name? Perhaps you returned the insult with, "Sticks and stones may break my bones, but words will never hurt me." I don't know about you, but those words *did* hurt me, and some comments stayed with me a long time. The spoken word is powerful; it can lift one to joyous heights or painfully crush the spirit.

Keep in mind your role as a battle buddy as you consider the following Scriptures.

"An anxious heart weighs a man down, but *a kind word cheers him up*" (Proverbs 12:25, emphasis mine).

"A man finds joy in giving an apt reply—and *how good is a timely word*" (Proverbs 15:23, emphasis mine)!

"*A word aptly spoken is like apples of gold* in settings of silver" (Proverbs 25:11, emphasis mine).

"*Pleasant words are* a honeycomb, *sweet* to the soul and *healing* to the bones" (Proverbs 16:24, emphasis mine).

People may forget the words you *say*, but they will never forget how those words made them *feel*.

With that in mind, here are some verbal *dos* and *don'ts* to remember.

Do say:

- "What do you think is a realistic weight for you? How can I help you reach that goal?"
- "Is there anything I can do to help you in your battle [right now, today, this week]?"
- "I sense you are discouraged; what can I do to help lift your burden?"
- "*We* suffered some setbacks today; what can *we* do to make tomorrow victorious?"

- "I can see you're making headway in your weight loss."
- "Your face and body language is reflecting your new character development." (Make godly character development rather than physical appearance the focus.)
- "I know you've struggled with dieting in the past, but this is a fresh approach I believe will make a difference."
- "I'm here for you *whenever* you need me!"

Don't say:
- "You don't need to lose any weight" or "Why would *you* want to lose weight?" (If your loved one has a weight problem, you both need to be honest and address it. If he or she is definitely *not* overweight and has a distorted bodily view, consider getting professional help through your physician and pastor.)
- "You'll never be able to lose weight. Look how many times you've failed in the past."
- "If you loved me, you would lose weight."
- "I would love you if you would just lose _____ pounds."
- "You can start tomorrow." (When your soldier has made the difficult decision to begin the battle, don't encourage delay.)
- "Lose it, or else." (No one likes feeling threatened. Your loved one needs support and encouragement, not ultimatums.)
- "Have just one" or "It's OK to eat _____ just this once." (Offering wrong food is giving your soldier an opportunity to fail, and it may foil the entire battle. Just as you would never offer a drink to a recovering alcoholic, don't offer wrong food to your loved one.)
- "I've been trying to help you for _____ months/years. If you don't lose weight this time, I'll never help you again." (Remember, this is a lifelong battle—for *both* of you!)

And now, valued battle buddy, may you be Lafayette to your Washington. May you fight side by side in battle, rejoice together in victory and cry together in defeat, and may the intimacy of your friendship last a lifetime.

Prayer for the Battle Buddy: Dear Lord, help me be the loving support my soldier needs, and to be especially sensitive to his or her emotional needs. Give me wisdom as

I choose my words, and show me areas in my own life where I can improve my eating habits. As I support my loved one, I commit to develop godly character in my personal battles. In Jesus' name, I pray. Amen.

Memory Verse: *"Carry each other's burdens, and in this way you will fulfill the law of Christ." Galatians 6:2*

Food for Thought

There are those who prefer to battle alone, but I believe God designed us to need the help and support of others. Battling together is an opportunity to share joys in victories and discouragements in defeats—to learn to bear one another's burdens. I know people who have been friends for years, but through our battle groups, their friendships have developed an entirely new depth and intimacy. I suggest you prayerfully consider starting your own battle group at your church or in your home. You can begin with as few as two "soldiers," or with any number you desire. The *Planning for the Battle of the Bulge* companion workbook/journal and *The Winning the Battle of the Bulge Leader's Guide* will help you facilitate your meetings.

COMMANDING OFFICERS: PRACTICING WHAT YOU PREACH

"For it is time for judgment to begin with the family of God."
1 Peter 4:17

CHAPTER FOURTEEN

Commanding Officers: Practicing What You Preach

"All right, you guys, turn that television off, and get busy!" I called to my children, Rachel, David, and Jonathan. "There are clothes lying all over your rooms, and we need to get this place picked up."

As if they hadn't heard me, three little faces stared straight ahead, and no one moved. They were hoping I'd go away.

"Hey!" I said louder and with more force. "You can watch TV *after* you clean up your rooms."

Facing the inevitable, they reluctantly dragged themselves off the couch and slumped toward their rooms. As Rachel reached her bedroom door, she turned to me and said, "Mom, how come *we* have to pick up our clothes, but Daddy doesn't have to pick up his?"

Rachel wasn't being rude or sassy; she was simply asking a legitimate question. Why were she and her brothers expected to do something their father did not have to do?

I opened and closed my mouth searching for an intelligent answer as all three kids looked at me, waiting.

My pathetic reply was, "You need to do what's right even if we don't. Now go clean your rooms!"

I was secretly pleased with my new ammunition, and I couldn't wait for Bill to get home that evening so I could tell him what Rachel had said. I had been asking—OK, *nagging*—him for fifteen years to pick up his clothes, to no avail. When he walked through the door that evening, I waited all of five seconds to tell him what his daughter had said. *So what do you have to say to that*, I thought triumphantly. I couldn't wait to hear the lame excuse he would offer.

He looked at me for a moment, and then said, "She's right."

That day Bill and I were reminded of three valuable leadership principles that we try to implement in our home and in our ministry.

1. **People do not respond to nagging in a positive way.** Rachel's observation and simple question accomplished what I had not been able to do in fifteen years of nagging. Occasionally, I could get Bill to pick up his clothes but by the following day, another pile would be started. Telling him what to do occasionally produced some results, but they were not long lasting. It was easier for him to leave the clothes on the floor, tune out my griping, and wait for me to eventually pick them up.

2.   **If you're wrong, admit it**. Bill could have made excuses for not picking up his clothes (to be honest, he had in the past), but he knew he was wrong and admitted it. Acknowledging wrong behavior is not a sign of weakness; it's a sign of good leadership.

3.   **If you really want to make an impact in another person's life, back up your words with your behavior**. In other words, practice what you preach! Bill knew he should pick up his clothes, but he wasn't motivated to do so until he realized his children were modeling his behavior.

I can truthfully say I've rarely picked up Bill's clothes since that day. He realized that his actions spoke to the kids far louder than words alone, and he made a conscious decision to change his behavior.

Nothing will destroy credibility in the home or the church faster than hypocrisy—*saying* one thing but *living* another. As church leaders, are you guilty like Bill and me? Do the people under your leadership feel you're telling them what to do, but you're not doing it yourself?

While doing research for this book, I conducted a survey on weight loss with nearly one hundred Christians from various denominations. Again, and again, people said they had trouble sitting under the leadership of a pastor or other church leader who was overweight. (One man went so far as to say he would not attend a church where the pastor was overweight.) When I asked why, the answer was always the same with slight variations. *I have a hard time listening to someone telling me to let God develop self-control in my life when it's obvious they haven't let him control their eating habits.*

Ouch! The truth hurts, doesn't it?

I know firsthand the unique pressures and temptations church leaders—pastors in particular—face when it comes to food. Sometimes it seems like the entire world revolves around a table stacked high with mouth-watering goodies. If food isn't served at Bible study or church, someone invites you out to a restaurant after services. You stop by a parishioner's home, and they offer you dessert. Girl Scouts sell cookies, and you must buy at least one box from each of the little green-clad girls who attend your fellowship. Sweet elderly ladies want to bless you with your favorite cookies or pie. Coffee and doughnuts are served between Sunday School and the worship service, and since there was no time for breakfast, you grab just one—or two—or three. The opportunities and temptations for overindulging are endless, and before you know it, you're carrying around an extra twenty-five pounds, then fifty!

A 1998 study by Purdue University professor Kenneth Ferraro found that Christians are more likely to be overweight than those persons of other faiths. Why? I believe the simple answer is that our recreational time and fellowship activities revolve around food, but the hard answer is that we have not developed discipline and self-control in the area of our eating and exercise habits.

Making a First Impression

My husband and I have been in ministry leadership positions for more than thirty years; we've known unspeakable joy and devastating hurt. Though rewarding, ministry is often difficult. You can do everything seemingly right and still people find fault with you. The men and women in ministry leadership positions are judged and scrutinized in every area—the model of cars they drive, the way their children behave, the cost of their homes, the brands of clothes they wear, and yes, even how much they weigh.

It would be nice if people got to know how wonderful and spiritual we are before they passed an opinion. But unfortunately, we are often first judged by our physical appearance. Indeed, sometimes our competence, personality, and spirituality are judged by how we look.

Two years after my husband accepted his first pastorate, one member told me she voted for Bill when he came to candidate because she thought we were an attractive young couple. I didn't say anything, but I thought, *What about our education and ministry experience? Didn't that count for anything?* Even though her opinion was positive, it disturbed me that our outward appearance had affected her judgment. But, I think there is a good lesson in her comment. We don't have to look like we stepped out of *Vogue* magazine, but our outer appearance should be neat and clean and reasonably up–to-date. In no way should our appearance detract from the message God wants to tell through us.

That's not right, you say. *Leaders shouldn't be judged more harshly than anyone else.* Perhaps, but right or not, it goes with leadership positions. As a ministry leader, don't you want someone's first impression of you, your church, and your ministry to be positive? And, before you criticize the critics, if you're honest, aren't you sometimes guilty of judging others by appearance and acting on first impressions?

Most pastors I know make sure their church buildings are painted and in good repair, the bathrooms and nursery are kept clean, and the yard is mowed and tended. Why? Because outward appearance matters; first impressions make a difference. We want people to look at our church and think, *I would like to visit that church. I can tell the people care.*

If your leadership position involves the morning worship service, you want the chairs straight, the ushers prepared, the musicians ready, the sound clear, and, most of all, no surprises. Why? You don't want anything to detract from the message!

If you're the church secretary, you want to make sure there are enough bulletins for everyone in the service and they are free of typos. Why? You don't want anything to detract from the message!

If you're in charge of the nursery, you want the workers to arrive on time and be ready to spend an hour *cheerfully* taking care of the babies and toddlers. Why? You don't want anything to detract from the message!

The outward condition of your church building and the organization of your church service is a direct reflection of the inward condition of the leadership, the congregation, *and* the Lord. Your *outward* condition is a direct reflection of your *inward* condition, too.

Why then, risk jeopardizing God's message with lack of self-control in your eating?

Making the Right Choice

"I speak to Christian and secular audiences that number in the thousands, and I know that in both arenas, the moment I walk onto the platform my weight detracts from my message," Jill told me matter-of-factly. "There are people sitting in the audience who take one look at me, and the first thought that goes through their head is *she is really fat.* They have to get over that hurdle before they can listen to what I say. I know God is using my message and me, but I also know he could do more through me if I could lose my excess weight. Please, can you tell me more about your eating program? I need help."

The evening before Jill and I had that conversation, I presented my book idea to fifty authors and speakers. Jill was one of six ladies (all but one considerably overweight) who sought me out and asked me to explain more about my book and program. Jill was well dressed, stylishly coifed, and had a beautiful face, yet she painfully acknowledged her weight was a detriment to her ministry.

Monica, another of the six women, shared her story with me. Several years earlier, she had counseled a teenage girl who was involved in a sexual affair. During one of the counseling sessions, the girl looked Monica straight in the face and said, "My problem is I'm having sex outside of marriage; *your problem is you're fat.* When you've taken care of *your* problem *then* you can come back and talk to me about mine!" Monica acknowledged her gluttony and lost more than fifty pounds.

You have a choice. You can either make excuses for your self-indulgence, call those who criticize *immature Christians,* and quote a few choice Bible verses. Or, you can say as Bill did when he was confronted by Rachel's question, "They're right," and do something about it. I hope you will make the right choice, just as you would expect of those under your leadership.

Challenges for Those in Leadership

Change begins at the top. Below are some challenges for those of you who have leadership influence in your congregations or groups—senior pastor, Sunday School teacher, sound person, maintenance worker, musician, office worker, or attendee. *Everyone is the leader of someone!*

- Lovingly address the issue of obesity in America and its prevalence in the church. One day I sat in church watching a delightful PowerPoint presentation by a visiting missionary couple, and I listened intently as they commented on each picture flashing across the screen. The slide show included photos of their worship center, home, and the fascinating tribal people to whom they minister. As a picture of the missionary couple was shown on the screen, the husband laughingly referred to himself, "And here's a picture of a fat missionary." I looked from the screen to the missionary and back again as I heard uneasy laughter scattered throughout the congregation. *Why*, I wondered, *does this man want to publicly bring attention to his very obvious weight problem? If he had a problem with alcohol, he wouldn't joke about that.* Obesity is *not* a laughing matter; it is a serious problem that touches a person physically, emotionally, and spiritually, and the church needs to address it.

- Knowing that the body of a believer is the temple of the Holy Spirit and belongs to the Lord (1 Corinthians 6:19-20), teach the inestimable value of exercise and eating healthy foods. We spend a great deal of time teaching about the *new* body we're going to have in heaven, but we don't take care of the *old* one we have here on earth.

- Encourage your members to prepare healthy meals at home and church. Church functions should not be an excuse for gluttony, but rather a time to enjoy sweet fellowship and God's gift of food in moderate portions. Christians should be an *example* to the world, not the object of jokes and ridicule.

- Encourage families to spend quality time together exercising their bodies, preparing and planning meals, and having fellowship at the dinner table. Too many families eat in front of the television or eat on the run because their lives are consumed with activities. Just as you encourage families to have devotions together, encourage them to take care of their bodies together.

- Be an example to your group. 2 Timothy 4:12 tells leaders to be an example to believers by the words they speak, the way they act, and the things they teach. Your actions will speak far louder than your words alone. Leading those in your group in obedience to the Lord by developing healthy eating and exercise habits will give you insight into their personal needs. You will be counseling, leading by example, learning and fighting side by side with your fellow soldiers.
- If you personally have a weight problem, acknowledge it, and take steps to fight your own battle. You will earn the respect of your people and help establish personal credibility while strengthening the effectiveness of your ministry. Don't allow Satan to use your weight to detract from the message of the gospel. People love a humble leader.
- Recognize that the unique pressures on leadership are major contributing factors in the vast number of overweight Christian leaders. The size of your group or congregation is in direct proportion to the number of individual expectations of each member. Unfortunately, whether that number is five or five hundred, you will have that number of opinions on how you should live your life and conduct your ministry. Learn to "cast all your anxiety on him because he cares for you" (1 Peter 5:7).
- Smoking and drinking alcohol are not acceptable forms of stress relief in most Christian circles; hence, people turn to food. Though God condemns gluttony along with drunkenness (Proverbs 23:20-21), the former has seemingly become socially acceptable in our churches, and often leaders are sad examples of its effects. Do not turn to food for comfort and release.
- If you don't have a weight problem, be compassionate toward those who do. Help guide them into a program that will provide encouragement and support. Teach and model that God is their defender, strength, and sufficiency in all battles, including their weight battle.

He Practices What He Preaches

I'd like to tell you about a man who I consider to be one of the greatest leaders of all time. *He practices what he preaches.* Like most churches, his group is made up of nearly all volunteers—untrained and unorganized volunteers. But, he is patient and appreciates each contribution made to the cause. He tries to spend as much time with his family as he possibly can, but often they experience separation because he believes God called him to lead, and he is passionate about his cause. Besides, he knows the folks in his group are making the same sacrifices. So, *he practices what he preaches.*

He lives in a beautiful home and loves working outdoors on his property, but that too must be put on hold for the sake of the cause. When funds are low, and his followers are discouraged, he gives from his personal resources to keep them going. They can see *he practices what he preaches.* Every person in his group has experienced serious trials and suffering, but they keep going because their leader suffers the same trials. They're resolute; *they* won't give up because *he* won't give up. *He practices what he preaches.*

They know he's not perfect, but they love him because they know he loves them in return, and they are unwavering in their loyalty—till death, if necessary. There are some on his staff who have been disloyal to him, but he will not retaliate, even though trustworthy staff members have advised him to fire the dissenters. That's God's job, he believes, and so, *he continues to practice what he preaches.*

Who is this man, this incredible church leader, this great pastor? He is not a church leader or pastor at all; his name is General George Washington, commander in chief of the Continental army. He was a great leader, not only because he led great men, but also because *he practiced what he preached.*

Church leaders, shall we do any less?

Prayer: Dear Lord, forgive me for the times I have not practiced what I preached. Help me lead those in my group to a better understanding of you and to teach them to treat their bodies with respect and gratefulness. Help me to be an example in my home. In Jesus' name, I pray. Amen.

Memory Verse: *"For it is time for judgment to begin with the family of God."* 1 Peter 4:17

Food for Thought

Review the *Challenges for Those in Leadership* with someone close to you and be accountable to each other as you lead those in your group.

ULTIMATE VICTORY

"'Where, O death, is your victory? Where, O death, is your sting?'
The sting of death is sin, and the power of sin is the law. But thanks
be to God! He gives us the victory through our Lord Jesus Christ."
1 Corinthians 15:55-57

CHAPTER FIFTEEN

Ultimate Victory

The young navy doctor felt a wave of helplessness as he stared in disbelief at the wounded soldiers being brought aboard the ship. The infirmary was long ago filled to capacity, and now the bodies were placed wherever they could find space. His classes in medical school had not prepared him for this kind of carnage. So many wounded; so many dying. The commanding generals had feared severe casualties, but nothing of this magnitude.

As the doctor made his way through the rows of bloodied bodies, he allowed his medical training to take over, and he rapidly began to assess the condition of each soldier. The ship's blood supply was already running alarmingly low, and he came to a horrifying realization—they would never have enough blood to save the lives of all the dying men. He would have to make the difficult choice of which soldiers to give the precious blood.

That young naval officer was my father-in-law, Dr. Ian D. Murphy, and the incident took place on June 6, 1944, off the beaches of Normandy, France.

During the first twenty-five years of my marriage, I rarely heard my father-in-law talk about his war years. The few stories he shared were mostly humorous anecdotes about treating fellow sailors on board ship when they were in the Pacific. But one spring day we sat in his living room, and he began to tell about his service on D-Day and the weeks following. Ian was in the early stages of Alzheimer's disease, and so each story he shared was a special gift to us. My husband, my children, and I sat transfixed as we listened to his heart-wrenching account.

I cried as Ian told of one soldier who looked pleadingly into his eyes, as if begging him to save his life. For some reason, this particular young man stood out in his memory, and after more than fifty years, it was obviously still painful. Ian told how he held the soldier's hand as the young man died, and there was nothing he could do to help. There wasn't enough blood to save him.

I've thought of that story many times in the last few years, particularly now that my father-in-law is gone. I can picture him in my mind as a young naval doctor desperately trying to save as many lives as he could.

I'm so thankful there is no shortage of blood when it comes to our Savior, the Lord Jesus Christ. His blood was sufficient to pay for the sins of every person in the entire world.

Missing the Boat

I was raised in the church, and perhaps that's why, for the first few years of my life, I missed the boat; I missed seeing the complete picture of Jesus' death on the cross. I heard about Jesus every week in Sunday School and church, and perhaps I took God and the Bible for granted. We sang songs about him, heard stories about him, colored pictures about him, and memorized Bible verses about him. I loved Jesus as a young child does, and I even told him I would be a missionary in Africa when I grew up. To me, that was the ultimate sacrifice.

I knew Jesus died on the cross, was buried, and arose to pay for my sins (my offenses against God), but I didn't think his payment was enough; I felt I needed to do something to deserve eternal life. I was baptized as an infant, and I tried hard to behave and do good works so God would be pleased with me and take me to heaven when I died. I tried to keep the Ten Commandments, be kind to others, and each night when I said my prayers, I asked God to forgive me for all the sins I had committed that day. I told him I would try to be perfect—starting tomorrow.

When I was in junior high school, my brother Carl asked me to go with him to a teen Bible study. Not wanting to attend the same social functions as my brother, I turned him down every week for three months. Finally, I said, "Carl, I will go with you one time if you promise not to *ever* ask me again." He agreed, and my life was changed.

That evening a man stood before us with his Bible and shared Scripture verses I'd never seen before. He showed us from Romans 3:23 that all of us are sinners. That made sense, since I knew I wasn't as perfect as God. Then he read, "For it is by grace you have been saved, through faith—and this not from yourselves, it is the gift of God—*not by works*, so that no one can boast" (Ephesians 2:8-9, emphasis mine).

For the first time in my life, I understood that Jesus Christ had died on the cross— yes, *shed his blood*—to *freely* give me eternal life. I had spent years trying to *work* for something God wanted to *give* me. The man explained that Jesus died for me, and if I would simply receive him by faith, I would spend eternity in heaven with God. I still had a few questions, but it began to make sense, and then he turned in his Bible to 1 John 5:13. For people like me who still had doubts, the Apostle John said, "I write these things to you who believe in the name of the Son of God [Jesus Christ] so that you may *know* that you have eternal life" (emphasis mine). That evening, I silently prayed to God and accepted his free gift through faith in Christ.

The Food that Satisfies Our Souls

Coming from a broken, troubled home, my decision was more than just an assurance of life after death; my new relationship with God filled a void. I realized God loved me unconditionally in spite of my sin. He didn't just promise me eternal life in heaven, but he promised me peace and contentment here on earth. He didn't promise a life void of pain and trouble, but *a life that he would satisfy.*

Throughout the first four books in the New Testament, Jesus taught his followers through stories and allegories. He used examples from everyday life so they would grasp the concepts he was trying to teach. Many of his stories, parables, and even his miracles, had to do with food such as figs, wheat, salt, fish, bread, water, and wine. These things were the substance of their lives—how they made their livings, how they survived; these were things they understood.

One day Jesus went to a well, and a woman from nearby Samaria came to draw water (John 4:5-26). Jesus began to tell her about a special kind of water he was giving away—better water than she could draw from the well. He called it living water and told her if she drank of it, she would never be thirsty again. He said this living water was freely given, and it would satisfy her forever. I wonder if the woman thought Jesus was teasing her, or perhaps she thought he was a little crazy. But the woman listened and, before long, she understood that the living water Jesus offered was eternal life through faith in him. The Samaritan woman knew what it meant to be emotionally thirsty. She had been married five times and, now unmarried, was living with another man. She had spent her life seeking to quench her emotional thirst with the love of men. Instead, she discovered *Jesus is the one who satisfies the thirsty soul.*

On another occasion, Jesus spoke to a large crowd by the Sea of Galilee (John 6:1-13). He had just miraculously fed more than five thousand people with just five loaves of bread and two small fish, and he knew the people were following him because of his miracles. He also knew their souls had a hunger only he could fill, so he freely offered them the bread of life. He explained that he himself was that bread of life, and if they would receive him by faith, they could have eternal life and never hunger again. The seeking crowd found *Jesus is the one who satisfies the hungry soul.*

The spiritual and emotional hunger we have in our souls can only be satisfied through a relationship with God, and that relationship comes through faith in Jesus Christ.

"Oh, that men would give thanks to the LORD for His goodness, And for His wonderful works to the children of men! *For He satisfies the longing soul, and fills the hungry soul with goodness*" (Psalm 107:8-9, emphasis mine).

Remember, *God-given appetites can only be satisfied with God-given gifts.*

The Enemy Deceives

Like so many others, I was deceived, caught unaware. I listened to Satan's subtle lies about my eternal future—lies that seemed to make sense.

Satan said: Nothing in life is free.

God said: "…But the *gift* of God is eternal life in Christ Jesus our Lord" (Romans 6:23, emphasis mine).

Satan said: You have to work your way to heaven.

God said: "…The *work* of God is this: to *believe* in the one [Jesus Christ] he has sent" (John 6:29, emphasis mine).

Satan said: Do it your own way.

God said: "…*I am the way* and the truth and the life. No one comes to the Father except through me" (John 14:6, emphasis mine).

Satan said: A blood sacrifice is a ridiculous way to pay for sin.

God said: "Knowing that you were not redeemed with corruptible things, like silver or gold…*but with the precious blood of Christ…*" (1 Peter 1:18-19, emphasis mine).

Satan said: It's too simple.

God said: "But I fear, lest somehow, as the serpent deceived Eve by his craftiness, so your minds may be corrupted from *the simplicity that is in Christ*" (2 Corinthians 11:3, emphasis mine).

That evening at the teen Bible study, I quit listening to Satan's lies and I accepted the Lord Jesus Christ as the one who died for me. *His blood was enough to pay for my sins; he gave me a complete transfusion.* His death and resurrection is the ultimate victory.

Prayer: Dear Lord, Thank you for sending Jesus to die on the cross to pay for my sins. Thank you that he arose from the dead and that he is a living Savior. Thank you that I don't have to listen to Satan's lies any longer. Please help me as I share this good news with others. In Jesus' name, I pray. Amen.

Memory Verse: *"'Where, O death, is your victory? Where, O death, is your sting?' The sting of death is sin, and the power of sin is the law. But thanks be to God! He gives us the victory through our Lord Jesus Christ." 1 Corinthians 15:55-57*

Food for Thought

Do you feel empty inside? Does your soul thirst and hunger for something, and you're not sure what it is? Are you trying to earn something that has already been paid for? Jesus Christ is the only one who can satisfy the hunger and thirst of your soul.

Perhaps you've never accepted God's free gift of eternal life. If not, would you do it right now? Simply pray something like this: "Lord, I don't understand it all, but I realize Jesus Christ died on the cross and arose again to freely give me eternal life. Right now, the best I know how, I'm receiving that gift by faith. Amen."

If you sincerely prayed that prayer, the Bible says you have eternal life *right* now.

"Most assuredly I say to you, he who believes in Me [Jesus Christ]
_____*has everlasting life. I am the bread of life" (John 6:47-48).*

If you are putting your faith in Christ to give you eternal life, please write your name in that space.

If you're trusting Christ as your Savior for the first time, or if you have questions about this chapter, I would like to hear from you. Please contact me at:

Mary@lookingglassministries.com

or

Mary Englund Murphy
Looking Glass Ministries
10632 South Memorial Drive
Suite 126
Tulsa, Oklahoma 74133

Battling for Life: Victorious for Eternity

"Therefore, since we are surrounded by such a great cloud of witnesses, let us throw off everything that hinders and the sin that so easily entangles, and let us run with perseverance the race marked out for us. Let us fix our eyes on Jesus, the author and perfecter of our faith, who for the joy set before him endured the cross, scorning its shame, and sat down at the right hand of the throne of God."
Hebrews 12:1-2

Chapter Sixteen

Battling for Life: Victorious for Eternity

Noah—the man who "...found grace in the eyes of the LORD" (Genesis 6:8). Noah—the man who "...when warned about things not yet seen, in holy fear built an ark to save his family. By his faith he...became heir of the righteousness that comes by faith" (Hebrews 11:7). Noah—the man who "...walked with God" (Genesis 6:9) while no doubt enduring ridicule from his friends and neighbors as he obediently built an ark in a world that had never seen rain. Noah—the man with whom God made a covenant and gave the rainbow as a sign of promise to never again destroy the earth by water. Noah—the man who started over as a farmer, harvested his vineyard, and drank himself into a stupor. *Noah—the man who forgot battling is for a lifetime.*

David—the young shepherd boy who killed a lion and a bear, and defeated the dreadful giant Goliath. David—the man who Samuel anointed king of Israel. David—the man who God protected and blessed as he ran from the wrath of King Saul. David—the man who wrote hundreds of encouraging songs that have endured for generations. David—the man God said had a heart like his own. David—the man who committed adultery and murder. *David—the man who forgot battling is for a lifetime.*

Peter—the man chosen by Christ as one of his twelve intimate companions and disciples. Peter—the man who witnessed and participated in the Messiah's innumerable miracles—turning water into wine, healing his own mother-in-law, the feeding of thousands, casting out demons, and raising the dead. Peter—the man who walked on water and saw Christ transfigured on a mountaintop. Peter—the man who denied his Savior three times in only one night. *Peter—the man who forgot battling is for a lifetime.*

After nine months of battling, I was within four pounds of my goal. I had faithfully stuck to my battle plan and was sharing with others in our battle groups. It had become such a fundamental part of my life that I thought I couldn't be defeated. I told myself that this battle thing was pretty easy and I could effortlessly maintain my weight. I began to let my guard down and I wasn't even aware of it. I no longer planned ahead for the eating battles I might encounter during the coming week, and I didn't feel the need to weigh in as often. Instead of drinking the one soda per week to which I committed, I treated myself to an extra one here and there. My helpings at the dinner table were a little larger, and I indulged in the desserts I previously pushed to the side. I began to make unguarded choices, and before I knew it, I gained five pounds, then ten. I had forgotten the war is not over when I reach my goal; *I had forgotten battling is for a lifetime.*

There are days, even weeks, I struggle with my former thinking and attitudes, and I find myself believing the same lies and falling into my old patterns. I have to remind myself the enemy is still attacking; he is still trying to rob God of his glory; he still wants me to fail. I have to remind myself that often the basis of my struggles is simply my own lusts and selfish desires to have my way. But, whatever the source, I know *I will fight my battle of the bulge for the rest of my life.*

Still Vulnerable

No matter how long you battle, no matter how proficient you are at weaponry, no matter how confident you become, you will always be vulnerable to emotional ups and downs and attacks from the enemy. In fact, you may be at your *most* vulnerable when you are near or when you reach your goal. Maintaining your focus will be an entirely new battlefield. Some attacks will be blatant, while others will be made with such subtlety you won't even be aware what's happening. Whatever the source of attack or the power of its strength, the purpose is always the same—to get you off track and to sever your focus on Christ.

Let's look at some of the reasons you might get off track.

- **You stop making daily battle plans**. This is probably the number one reason people in our battle groups quit, or see little progress. Daily planning and accountability is vital in any battle, particularly to professional dieters who find it easy to nibble during meal preparation, snack without thinking, and add a little (or a lot) extra to their food helpings. *The Planning for the Battle of the Bulge* companion workbook/journal can be a great resource in your war, affording opportunity for accountability and daily Bible reading.

  Remember: Battling is for life, and that includes preparing a plan for each day. When your life is through, you will want to say with the Apostle Paul, "I have fought the good fight, I have finished the race, I have kept the faith" (2 Timothy 4:7).

- **You lose sight of your goal**. As friends and loved ones begin to notice your weight loss, the temptation will be to start thinking more about your physical appearance than the obedience that brings glory to Christ. It's natural to enjoy compliments and attention, but when outward appearance becomes your primary motivation, your focus will be self-centered and shallow.

Remember: Paul told the Philippians, "I press toward the goal for the prize of the upward call of God in Christ Jesus" (Philippians 3:14).

- **You are distracted by unexpected circumstances in your life.** Unexpected circumstances sometimes bring unwelcome change, but eating for comfort is *not* the answer. The enemy will tell you it's all right to cheat this once because you deserve it, and it will make you feel better. Besides, you can always make up for it later, right? No! You must keep your focus on obedience to the moment.

  Remember: Though you may start again tomorrow, *you have only this moment to be obedient to this battle.* "…Has the LORD as great delight in burnt offerings and sacrifices, as in obeying the voice of the LORD? Behold, to obey is better than sacrifice…" (1 Samuel 15:22).

- **Satan has changed his strategy or he is attacking other areas of your life.** The enemy does not want you to succeed. As you discover and use the right weapons for your battle, he will try to make you fail by changing his tactics and area of attack.

  Remember: Your enemy is cunning and wicked (Ephesians 6:11-12), he is a liar (John 8:44), and he wants to devour you (1 Peter 5:8).

- **You need to continue developing godly character.** Character growth never stops and, unfortunately, is usually accompanied by trials and tribulations. Just when you think you have all the character you need, you will face another unforeseen situation that will require new growth. The good news is each character quality you develop in your battle of the bulge can be used in other battles.

  Remember: "His divine power has given us everything we need for life and godliness through our knowledge of him who called us by his own glory and goodness" (2 Peter 1:3).

- **You have let down your guard.** Battling requires you to be vigilant at all times. It's easy to make an occasional unguarded choice—skipping your daily devotions, increasing your portion sizes, eating late night snacks, licking the mixing bowl, finishing the kids' leftovers, or sampling food while you cook. Compromise in little things is the first step toward total disobedience.

Remember: The soldier who is vigilant will not be caught by a surprise attack. "…Be watchful in all things…" (2 Timothy 4:5).

- **You are allowing your emotions to control you.** You will have times of anger, frustration, and discouragement, but *you* control how you respond to your emotions. Eating to satisfy an emotional whim will leave you frustrated and discontent.

    Remember: Through the power of the Holy Spirit you control your responses and choices. "Like a city whose walls are broken down is a man who lacks self-control" (Proverbs 25:28).

- **You're not losing weight as fast as you'd like.** During your weight-loss battle you will hit plateaus—times when you're being obedient but the pounds aren't coming off. This is the time to keep your focus on your primary goal: to glorify Christ through the transforming of your life and the renewing of your mind.

    Remember: Plateaus can be times of immense growth—*don't give up!* "And let us not grow weary while doing good, for in due season we shall reap if we do not lose heart" (Galatians 6:9).

Getting Back on Track

Everyone experiences setbacks from time to time. Usually these setbacks will amount to minor diversions, but some threaten to permanently derail you. If and when you find your focus is diverted, it's important to get back on track as quickly as possible. It will help if you periodically reevaluate your progress, strategies, and objectives to keep them fresh in your mind. (As you get close to your goal weight, you may discover that the amount you wanted to lose is unrealistic, and that you need to adjust your goals and objectives.) As you grow spiritually and emotionally in your relationship with Christ, the adjustments you need to make will become clear.

Changes in one's circumstances create new battles and can have a major effect on the weight-loss process. In the first four years after beginning my battle of the bulge, our youngest child left home for college, I began a high-pressured part-time job, and I began speaking and traveling more often. I didn't have time to prepare meals as I did when the kids were home, so we had to make adjustments in our menu. We also faced an emotional upheaval when Bill accepted a pastorate in another state, resulting in a major move for our family. In just over a year, Bill's father and my stepfather passed away, and we moved my ninety-one-year-old mother to live near us. The temptation to eat for emotional comfort was strong. Our physical needs were changing, too, as we began to experience middle-age health issues. Fortunately, I was learning to apply the battling principles in the new situations in my life and was able to gain the victory.

When you find yourself wavering, you may find it helpful to ask yourself the following questions:

- Am I having my daily devotional and prayer time?
- Am I preparing and following my daily battle plan?
- Am I allowing anything to divert my focus?
- Do I need a medical checkup?
- Am I staying accountable to at least one person weekly?
- Am I making poor strategic choices?
- Do I need to reevaluate my goals and motives?

You may also find it helpful to go back and read all or parts of this book. When I become complacent or self-focused or I divert from my purpose, I reread what I've written, and I'm encouraged to resume the battle.

Some Final Thoughts

I'm often asked if I think God has a specific weight he wants each of us to maintain, and my answer is, *I really don't know*. I do think he wants us to attain and maintain a *healthy* weight, and that figure will likely fluctuate by a few pounds depending on water gain, vacations, holidays, and other circumstances. What I think God is more interested in is establishing an ongoing personal relationship of fellowship between him and us. He wants our lives to praise, worship, and glorify him in every area.

Satan wants just the opposite. I don't think he cares how much we weigh as long as we remain self-absorbed; I don't think he cares what we think about as long as it's not God. Satan wants to divert praise, worship, and glory away from the Lord, and if he can do that by consuming our thoughts and actions with food and gluttony, he has accomplished his purpose. Overweight and, for that matter, grossly underweight Christians are just an added bonus for the enemy, because health and energy levels suffer as well as their testimony.

Fat or thin, a person's behavior may be equally gluttonous and wrong. I know people who don't have a problem with weight gain and eat anything and everything they desire, but just because they are thin doesn't mean they are eating good food and taking care of their bodies. The Scriptures say, "For the drunkard and the glutton will come to poverty..." (Proverbs 23:21) and "...put a knife to your throat if you are a man given to gluttony" (Proverbs 23:2).

Obese or emaciated, needing to lose ten or a hundred pounds, the same battle principles apply. It may, in fact, be more difficult for the person with a minimal amount of weight to lose because the tendency will be to do it entirely in his or her own power. Obviously, there is a vast difference in the size of the people, but the real difference is primarily in the number of pounds that need to be lost. Each person needs to obey day by day; each person needs to be broken; each person may be obsessed with weight and appearance; each person may suffer depression; and, each person needs maintenance for life.

No matter what your specific battles, you must take each one to the Lord, seek his guidance, and apply his answer. No two people in our groups follow the exact same plan. Some use guidelines from balanced diet books, some have medical issues that require strict dietary guidelines from a doctor, and some follow a commercial plan. You will have your ups and downs, your victories and defeats, but remember God is faithful and compassionate, and his mercies are new every morning (Lamentations 3:22-23).

Why not start today anew?

"I have not yet begun to fight!"

In December 1775, Scottish born John Paul Jones joined forces with the rebels of the American Revolution. After his commission in the Continental navy, he began raids against English shipping. On September 23, 1779, as commander of the French vessel the *Bon Homme Richard*, Jones engaged in a bloody sea battle against Richard Pearson, captain of the HMS *Serapis*. Badly damaged and with great loss of firepower, the *Bon Homme Richard* began to take on water. Pulling the *Serapis* within hearing distance, Captain Pearson called out to Jones, asking him to surrender. Jones famously replied, "I have not yet begun to fight!" With their ship literally sinking beneath them, Jones and his crew fought on until at last, Pearson and the crew of the *Serapis* surrendered.

When you are wounded and bloodied, and when you feel you can't be obedient even one more time, remember your purpose and the God you are serving. When the enemy calls for your surrender, in God's strength answer back, *"I have not yet begun to fight!"*

Prayer: Dear Lord, I know there will be times when I try to fight in my own strength and for my own purposes. Remind me who my enemy is, and that by your death, burial, and resurrection you have defeated him. Remind me I am victorious in you, and you will give me all the strength, power, and weapons I need to win my battle of the bulge. In Jesus' name, I pray. Amen.

Memory Verse: *"Therefore, since we are surrounded by such a great cloud of witnesses, let us throw off everything that hinders and the sin that so easily entangles, and let us run with perseverance the race marked out for us. Let us fix our eyes on Jesus, the author and perfecter of our faith, who for the joy set before him endured the cross, scorning its shame, and sat down at the right hand of the throne of God." Hebrews 12:1-2*

Food for Thought

On the days you think your battles are under control and the enemy is permanently defeated, and when you are trying to battle in your own strength, it will be then that God will patiently draw you back to himself and remind you to seek his face. He will remind you true victory is found only in obedience to him.

When I interviewed my friend Don for insight into boot camp, he gave me an additional valuable nugget involving his childhood. Each morning when he left the house for school, his parents said, "Remember who you are. Remember who you belong to."

I'd like to leave you with that challenge. If you have placed your faith in Christ, you are a child of the Almighty God of the universe, *victorious for eternity*. Why not live like it?

Remember who you are. Remember who you belong to.

"I thank my God every time I remember you. In all my prayers for all of you, I always pray with joy because of your partnership in the gospel from the first day until now, being confident of this, that he who began a good work in you will carry it on to completion until the day of Christ Jesus.

"It is right for me to feel this way about all of you, since I have you in my heart; for whether I am in chains or defending and confirming the gospel, all of you share in God's grace with me. God can testify how I long for all of you with the affection of Christ Jesus.

"And this is my prayer; that your love may abound more and more in knowledge and depth of insight, so that you may be able to discern what is best and may be pure and blameless until the day of Christ, filled with the fruit of righteousness that comes through Jesus Christ—to the glory and praise of God" (Philippians 1:3-11).

CHAPTER SEVENTEEN

BATTLING TIPS

*"Wisdom is supreme; therefore get wisdom. Though
it cost all you have, get understanding."*
Proverbs 4:7

CHAPTER SEVENTEEN

Battling Tips

This chapter is a gift to you the reader from the battle groups that have met over the last few years. Each week we shared ideas that helped us. These weapons (tips) are not necessarily original with our groups; some have come from books, magazine articles, lectures, or other sources. All the ideas will not necessarily apply to your battle. Feel free to add your own tips to the list.

- Always keep victory in sight. You *are* victorious in Christ!
- Don't boast as you lose weight. Remember who gets the glory.
- Pray often.
- Don't reward yourself with food. Your primary reward should be the satisfaction of obedience to the Lord, *then* the rewards of losing weight, better health, an expanded wardrobe, and renewed energy and strength. Think of other creative ways to reward yourself: bubble bath, movie, video game, or book.
- Celebrate each new victory with praise.
- As you lose weight, you will need to buy new clothes. Buy your "in-between" clothes at garage sales or thrift stores.
- Be prepared for criticism. Some people will not understand the process you are going through.
- Picture food as a gift. When it's healthy and in moderate portions, you can accept it as a gift from God. *Don't accept "gifts" from the enemy.*
- Brush your teeth and floss immediately after supper. It will give your mouth a fresh feeling and discourage you from eating again.
- Put extra food away *before* you sit down to eat your meals. It will discourage second helpings.
- Weigh each Friday and Monday to hold yourself accountable over the weekend.
- Record your weight at least weekly; your memory can play tricks on you.
- Use skin-firming lotion as you lose weight.
- Keep your food in a cabinet separate from the rest of the family. Don't open their cabinets.

- Take healthy snacks—carrots, apples, celery, nuts, berries, veggies, fruit—to work in an insulated lunch box.
- At a party or buffet, sit away from the food table to remove temptation.
- Avoid eating alone or in front of the television.
- Be prepared for people to say nothing about your weight loss. Some people will be jealous, and some people won't be sure if you've really lost weight and they will be too embarrassed to ask. Others are simply oblivious.
- Keep busy, but not so busy that you don't have time to plan. When you're idle, you have a tendency to fill your time with empty activities.
- Limit dressings, food toppings, and condiments. They can be loaded with sugar, and unwanted calories will add up before you know it.
- Avoid sugared and artificially sweetened beverages and those high in caffeine.
- After eating, wait a few minutes to see if you really *need*, not *want*, more food. Get up and do something to take your mind off the food. You can always come back and have a snack later.
- When someone insists that you eat food you shouldn't eat, say, "Thank you, but I can't eat that. I'll accept the gift but not the guilt."
- Don't blame others when you suffer a defeat. Learn to take responsibility for your actions.
- Weigh every day if it works as a goal reminder for you.
- Always weigh at the same time of day.
- Recite *out loud* encouraging verses throughout the day. It's hard to chew food and quote Scripture at the same time.
- Include your family and friends in your battle.
- Order from the children's menu when you eat in a restaurant.
- Face negative people with truth. You can't always remove negative people from your life, but you can limit the amount of time you spend with them.
- Tip at least 15 percent when you go out to eat; it is part of a good Christian testimony. If you share a meal, remember the waiter still served two people, so tip accordingly. *If you can't afford to tip, you can't afford to eat out.* (Many waiters don't like to work on Sundays because Christians are notorious for bad tipping.)
- When you think you want to "go on leave" from your battle of the bulge, think

about the consequences. Write them down so you can visualize them.

- Preplan your menu, and write it down so you'll have it when you come home from work tired.
- When you feel like eating a snack, drink a glass of water first and wait five minutes.
- Realize there are times when you will have to stand alone.
- Try not to eat on the run. If this is a common practice in your life, reevaluate your priorities. Ask: Is this necessary? What changes do I need to make?
- Remember to fight battles in advance. Keep your workbook/journal handy and check it frequently.
- Check out the New Food Pyramid at www.mypyramid.gov for tips and guidelines to healthy eating.

Exercise

- Consult your doctor or a certified physical trainer for a good program. If you experience discomfort, pain, or shortness of breath, contact your doctor immediately.
- Don't make excuses for not exercising. Instead, think of creative exercises for the times and places available to you.
- Don't compare your routine with someone else's. Create a program that is reasonable for your time schedule and your personal physical capabilities.
- Start slow and build up to a more challenging workout.
- Walking is a great exercise for almost everyone.
- Try to include your family or friends. It's more fun to exercise with another person.
- Combine exercise with other activities in your life: prayer, talking on the telephone, watching television, walking the dog, raking leaves, etc.
- Park away from store entrances and businesses to add a few extra steps.
- Exercise in small amounts throughout the day.
- Take the stairs instead of the elevator.
- Walk around the field during halftime at your kids' sporting events or while

you're watching them practice.

- Exercise with your kids, especially toddlers. Make a game of it.
- Don't have the time or the money to join a gym? Make use of public pools and parks.
- Remember the warm-up exercises you did in physical education class? Those are good exercises to do at home throughout the day.
- Don't want to exercise at the gym alone? Pick up an exercise video at a garage sale.

Memory verse: *"Wisdom is supreme; therefore get wisdom. Though it cost all you have, get understanding." Proverbs 4:7*

BATTLING ON THE FRONTLINE: SOLDIERS' STORIES

"And the things that you have heard from me among many witnesses, commit these to faithful men who will be able to teach others also."
2 Timothy 2:2

CHAPTER EIGHTEEN

Battling on the Frontline: Soldiers' Stories

I've been privileged to teach the principles and concepts in this book for several years. The principles and concepts are not mine, for they are found in the Word of God. I know they work because I've seen lives literally transformed as people discover their battle *isn't just about the weight*, but rather transformation of their minds through moment-by-moment obedience to Christ.

The following stories are from men and women who have been in a battle group and/ or have read my manuscript. I hope you are encouraged by their stories.

Vikki Robinson (20 pounds)

Through the message Mary has shared in her book and class on battling I have not only learned more about the battles we face every day in our Christian walk, but I have learned to stand, and *stand firm*! I have a deeper understanding of my commander in chief, and how developing godly character adds to my spiritual growth.

When starting this study, I was battling my weight problem. But the Lord showed me other areas where I had given up, retreated, or even been taken captive. I discovered *it's not just about the weight*. Through his Word, I have become a better soldier and have been able to use His battle plans to make a difference in my entire life.

Kim Floyd (70 pounds)

I believe this book is designed by God. It has been a tool he has used to redirect my focus away from me and the weight (because *it's really not just about the weight*), to focus on him. The character development in this book is unlike anything I have ever read or experienced. As I've strived and desired to be more obedient to Him by listening to His will for me, the consequences have been phenomenal. I've lost over seventy pounds. My life is more orderly and I have a closer relationship with my Lord, which is not always easy with home-schooling five young kids. I've watched the Lord work supernaturally through this program by watching how He uses it uniquely with each one in the class. I am so grateful to him for his love for me.

Melody Newman (35 pounds)

I've been on and off diets my entire adult life. I would lose weight, lose my motivation, go off the diet, feel like a failure, eat to make myself feel better, gain the weight back—plus some—and feel worse than I did before I started. It was a downward spiral, and I ended up more than seventy-five pounds overweight.

Then Mary invited me to join a group of Christian women who looked at weight loss in a different way. I didn't have much hope, but I went. I learned overeating was part of an ongoing war, and to be victorious, we needed to recognize our enemy, prepare for battle, and obey God, our commander in chief. Again and again, I heard these women say, "It's not just about the weight!" I didn't understand at first, but after much prayer and many battles, *I got it*! My weight was a symptom of a self-indulgent life with food as an idol. I realized if I could make God the focus of my life, my obsession with my weight would be removed.

I still struggled, but with God's help, my husband's encouragement, and the love and support of the battle group, I made progress. I changed my way of thinking, changed my eating habits, and began an exercise program. I've kept thirty-five pounds off for one year. I am not yet at my goal weight, but I have not "mustered out" of the army.

I've since been diagnosed with asthma complicated by a recurring pulmonary infection. This has created new battles. I have to find new ways to exercise and the medications make my weight battle more difficult. But the lessons I learned in *The Battle of the Bulge* have served me well. I know that just like the weight battle, my commander in chief fights by my side. He is in every breath I struggle to take. Just as I learned *it's not just about the weight*, I've also learned it's not about the asthma. It's about learning that the same Father, who helps me fight my overeating battles, helps me fight the whole war!

The war is life long, and will not be over until I am with my Lord in Heaven. But I know that Jesus is with me through it all, and when I do reach my goals, the victory is his.

Linda Payne (28 pounds)

I have battled my weight since I was a child and have tried every way and means to lose weight. *The Battle of the Bulge* has helped me to be honest in recognizing my problem and leading me to God's way to lose weight, maintain it, and develop a closer walk with him. This study will help people, not only in weight loss and maintenance, but in the other areas of life where Satan has control. The battles you win defeat Satan. It is a continuous war.

Sharon Clark (15 pounds)

It's not just about the weight! Weight loss is a by-product of walking in and living in the image of our commander in chief. Diligence, determination, commitment, integrity, steadfastness, faithfulness, self-control, and unselfishness are just some of the character qualities I've learned through my battle of the bulge. They are also necessary weapons to battle our way through the trials we face in this life. The promises in God's Word give us the strategy to combat our anxiety and our boredom, to find our contentment in our Lord. Addictions (whatever they may be) as comfort and contentment are only a band-aid. Only God can mend the wounds and fill our empty hearts with His gracious love. Only He can quench our appetites with the gifts he so freely gives. My goal is to reflect the character qualities of my revered commander in chief.

Bill Johnson (32 pounds)

I obsessed about food most of the time. As a recovering alcoholic, this was a behavior pattern I was used to. I had no battle plan whatsoever in place, so by mealtime I ate more than my share. I now realize eating can be battled on the home front. I learned in our group that my strategy has to be planned out ahead of time. This planning includes more than just filling my stomach with anything and everything, it also includes planning for proper snacks.

The most important thing I've learned is that I'm not alone in the war against being overweight. I'm losing weight, and with God on my side, we can win the battle of the bulge. I now think what the future has in store, as my relationship with God has grown.

Judy Kitchen (5 pounds)

I've always struggled with my weight, but particularly with accepting the way my body is shaped. I never liked the way I looked and for years tried to lose weight, thinking that would make a difference. But no matter how much weight I lost, my body was still the same pear shape.

Attending the *Winning the Battle of the Bulge* group gave me a new freedom in how I think about my body. I've learned to accept my frame because it's how God made me, and my body is the temple of the Holy Spirit. God has given me this body to serve him here on earth, and I need to take good care of myself. When I look in the mirror now, I tell myself I look good and thank God for the gift of my body. I find I'm taking the focus off myself and the way I look and am focusing on the things the Lord wants me to focus on.

Penny Wyllie (3 dress sizes)

Wow! I love the program! What a whole new way of looking at things. It is not focusing on weight. After fifty different "diets" and losing and gaining seventy-five pounds for thirty years, finally a solution that depends only on my relationship with the Lord. Dieting and denying myself certain foods was all about *me*. I have prayed repeatedly for God to simply change my eating habits to no avail. To depend on him, work with Him, and act according to how he wants me to act in my eating behavior appears to be the answer to my prayers—not my way or will, but his.

I love the daily Scripture readings and questions in the workbook/journal—somehow, they are perfect. They have gotten me more interested in Bible reading than anything I have done before. I don't concentrate on weight or weight loss or eating. I concentrate and think and pray on the character quality for the week, and leave the other alone. The character development is so important because they apply in every facet of your life, even in the little things like waiting in line.

Eating healthy and stopping when I am full is working. I'm convinced this is the only way I will ever lose weight and keep it off. My own willpower can get it off occasionally, but cannot keep it off or change my eating behavior lifestyle.

Robyn Butler

This class was my first real effort to control my eating. I'd never had any trouble keeping my weight under control before, but a thyroid condition and a heart attack made healthy eating mandatory. Mary showed me all kinds of pitfalls and mistaken beliefs about weight loss. Sometimes I'd laugh at myself for starting to do the very thing she had warned about the week before. Now I'm training my teenage daughters to have a godly attitude toward food and weight loss from the beginning. Best of all, no matter what my weight is, I'm content that my body is perfect for what God designed it to be. Healthy eating is a result of how obedient I am to God, not an attempt to boost my vanity and pride.

LaDonna Thornton (20 pounds)

I have struggled with my weight all of my life. I have tried every type of weight-loss device that is out on the market today. I've not found anything as helpful as Mary's book. She has taken something that's been so difficult for me and opened my eyes to the truth. I have taken the full class one time and it didn't sink in until the end. So, I'm ready to take it again and put everything into action. I'm so excited to see what God is going to do.

Mary Anderson (74 pounds)

Tipping the scales at close to 250 pounds, I began to limp. Walking became painful, and I couldn't climb stairs without getting winded. My job as a registered nurse required walking, climbing, and lifting as I cared for in-home health patients. I thought I would have to quit my job (a major portion of the income for my family), and I could see myself in a wheelchair. I sought medical treatment, but knew in my heart that without losing weight, treatments and exercise were only stopgap measures until everything would fall apart. I was getting desperate.

Diets? I'd been on some. I'd lose weight, keep it off, then feeling controlled and obsessed by having to think about what *not* to eat all the time, and I would give up.

Then Mary Murphy came to town, and I started going to the battle group in our church. I went because the people there were Christians and they were my friends. I was excited, and I was determined this would be the answer. It *was* the answer, but not the one I expected.

I learned I didn't know how to go about losing weight. When I tried before, I did it *my* way. I learned the battle was won first in preplanning, then in being obedient to the plan God helped me put together. The goal wasn't just to lose weight; it was to glorify God in how I was living. "So whether you eat or drink or whatever you do, do it all for the glory of God" (1 Corinthians 10:31), became a guide for each encounter with food. The tools, especially the *Planning for the Battle of the Bulge* companion workbook/journal for daily planning, have been a great help. The class was the accountability I needed. Slowly, the weight came off. I've lost seventy-four pounds (I still have thirty pounds to reach my goal). I've begun to feel good, I have energy, and my heels stopped hurting.

I have days that I'm enabled to use the strength of the Lord to win the battle. Other days—well, I'm not always successful. My focus isn't on the lost battles, but on the results that build my character. My lifestyle is changing and that change in me is permanent. As a work in progress, God keeps teaching me more about himself and how I am to transform my thinking and my character to be more like his Son, Jesus.

Lee Weeden (58 pounds)

Our lifestyle has totally changed from that of our forefathers. Men used to do hard labor from sunup to sundown, but not anymore. Now it's work eight hours (mostly in front of a computer) and then go home. However, our way of eating and the amount we eat has not adjusted to this lifestyle, and we eat out more often.

Over a period of three to four years, I gained over seventy-five pounds. I didn't feel good, and I knew I was not being a good testimony for Christ. I blamed my physical condition on the stress of work.

When I decided to start losing weight, I couldn't find a program that made sense, one I could stay on for any length of time. Then, I began to go to the battle weight-loss group at our church and lost twenty pounds. Two months later, I had a massive heart attack, and I really got serious. I went to rehab at the hospital, and now I exercise an hour daily and continue to watch what and how much I eat. I've also learned how important water is to our diet, and I drink sixty to eighty ounces each day.

God has shown me a different way of life. From a man's point of view, this weight-loss program with obedience to God as the focus is the only one that makes sense.

Diane Aniol (14 pounds)

When I first started hearing about the Battle of the Bulge group, I didn't think it was for me. I needed to lose a few pounds, but didn't want to go on a diet. But, I decided to go to the battle class at our church. What a concept! I could still cook, bake, and eat! I learned portion control and also to remember God's food satisfies my appetite, whether it is his physical food or his Spiritual food (his Word). Being satisfied with smaller portions and focusing on the food God has given to us in abundance has changed my outlook. I can even enjoy my desserts, whether one bite or a small piece. In fact, I enjoy desserts more, since I don't eat them all the time and I actually taste them now.

The class brought me to the realization that we cannot go without the right foods for our bodies and carry out God's plan with the stamina he wants from us.

The most important lesson I've learned is that the Christian walk is a battle! Our enemy, the devil, wants us to fail in everything we do. If we do not have our spiritual food every day and talk with God everyday, we cannot win our battles. God's Word satisfies my needs, the answers are there waiting for me to take and use. Battles are going to always be there, but with God as my commander in chief, I will win!

Memory verse: *"And the things that you have heard from me among many witnesses, commit these to faithful men who will be able to teach others also." 2 Timothy 2:2*

ACKNOWLEDGMENTS

There are not enough words or space to thank all those who have made this book a reality. It has been a journey I could not have completed without the prayers, help, and encouragement of my faithful friends and family.

My first group of battle buddies—Vikki Robinson, Sharon Clark, Gail Peterson, Linda Payne, Brenda Thayer, Melody Newman, Brenda Ledall, Elaine Colson, and Joni Kaiser. Thank you for sticking with me and for proving the truths of God's Word.

Dan and Gloria Penwell—Thank you for seeing what others did not see and for showing me what to do each step of the way.

Jeannie St. John Taylor—Thank you for graciously taking all my phone calls and for giving wise advice.

My first Tulsa battle group—Jim and Mary Anderson, Kim Floyd, Bill and Chris Johnson, Judy Kitchen, Robyn Butler, Lee and Dorla Weeden, Maxine Masters, Greg Floyd, Neva Berg, Carrie Ray, Charlotte McGowen, Teresa Nelson. Thank you for being my guinea pigs.

Thank you to the people of Calvary Bible Church, Tulsa, Oklahoma for your patience, encouragement, and support.

And, a very special thank you to Florence Littauer and Marita Littauer and the lovely staff at CLASServices (classervices.com). This book would not have happened without your vision, encouragement, training, mentoring, and direction. You are a *CLASS-y* bunch!

If the books *Winning the Battle of the Bulge: It's Not Just About the Weight* and *Planning for the Battle of the Bulge Companion Workbook/Journal* have been an encouragement to you, I would love to hear your story. Please write to me at...

Mary Englund Murphy
10632 South Memorial Drive, Suite 126
Tulsa, Oklahoma 74133

info@LookingGlassMinistries.com

...and include the information below:

Name Miss/Mrs./Mr. _____

Date _____

Address _____

City _____ State _____ Zip _____

Phone (   ) _____

E-mail address _____

❑ You have my permission to publicly share my story in your speaking and writing.

❑ You may use my first and last name.

❑ You may use my first name only.

❑ Change my name and the details of my story to protect my identity.

Establishing a Weekly Battle Group Bible Study

Are you interested in starting a weekly *Winning the Battle of the Bulge* battle group in your church or home? It's easier than you think. The battle groups are formatted for a one-hour time slot, so they may fit in to a small group or Sunday School setting.

Here's what you will need:
One person to facilitate thirteen weekly meetings.
A *Winning the Battle of the Bulge* leader's packet.
A *Winning the Battle of the Bulge* book and a *Planning for the Battle of the Bulge Workbook/Journal* for each person attending the class.

The leader's packet and books are available through Looking Glass Ministries and will be discounted for groups of ten or more.

Mary is also available to speak and help motivate your group as you begin your Bible study. She has developed a one-day seminar to launch your battle group and assure that everyone will get the most out of their thirteen-week commitment. A training session for group leaders is also included.

To order books and learn more about starting a group contact:
Mary Englund Murphy
Looking Glass Ministries
10632 South Memorial Drive
Suite 126
Tulsa, OK 74133

918-254-2410

LookingGlassMinistries.com

Mary@LookingGlassMinistries.com

Mary Englund Murphy

Mary knows whereof she writes. After battling with weight problems for many years, she learned and applied a Scriptural approach to weight control. She leads weight loss groups using her book *Winning the Battle of the Bulge* and teaches and trains others to lead groups in their churches.

She is the founder of Looking Glass Ministries, and she has been a keynote speaker at numerous seminars, retreats, banquets, and other events throughout the United States.

Mary and her husband Bill make their home in Tulsa, Oklahoma where Bill pastors Calvary Bible Church. They have three grown children Rachel, David, and Jonathan.

Mary is available to speak to your group on a variety of subjects. Contact her through LookingGlassMinistries.com or 918-254-2410.